IS AMERICAN DEMOCRACY EXPORTABLE?

The Insight Series:

Studies in Contemporary Issues

from The Glencoe Press

Problems of American Foreign Policy
Martin B. Hickman

The Oppenheimer Affair:
A Political Play in Three Acts
Joseph Boskin and Fred Krinsky

The Politics of Religion in America
Fred Krinsky

The Welfare State:
Who is My Brother's Keeper?
Fred Krinsky and Joseph Boskin

Opposition Politics:
The Anti-New Deal Tradition
Joseph Boskin

Is American Democracy Exportable?
Edward G. McGrath

Protest from the Right
Robert A. Rosenstone

Democracy and Complexity:
Who Governs the Governors?
Fred Krinsky

Ferment in Labor
Jerome Wolf

Series Editors: Fred Krinsky and Joseph Boskin

IS AMERICAN DEMOCRACY EXPORTABLE?

Edward G. McGrath

Department of Political Science
Oregon State University

THE GLENCOE PRESS
A Division of The Macmillan Company
Beverly Hills

 The Glencoe Press, A Division of the Macmillan Company. Collier-Macmillan Canada, Ltd., Toronto, Ontario. Library of Congress Catalog Card Number: 68-15573. *First Printing.*

Preface

No easy answer will be found to the question which serves as title of this book, nor will any single academic discipline supply a wholly satisfactory answer. The question for Americans is particularly unsettling. Each reader, in what he chooses to defend in our political tradition, will invariably illustrate his own desire to satisfy some personal ideal, some value, some interest, and these will all differ in form, time, and circumstance. Although there are a variety of defensible answers, some will certainly have more merit than others. It is an important objective then that the reader be stimulated and challenged to find the best possible answer.

Beyond their intrinsic value, the articles reprinted here expose a rich variety of working propositions which invite evaluation by critical thinking, comparative contextual analysis, and the methods of the social sciences. After a preliminary examination of the essential tenets of American democracy, the reading materials are organized according to topical subdivisions: American democracy as revolutionary experience, as mission, as a principle, as a modernizing influence, as a context for industrial civilization; finally, there is a discussion of the Peace Corps as a contemporary test case. The appeal throughout is to both humanists and behavioralists; the course of the American struggle for a better world depends on the efforts of all students of man and society.

This book should prove useful in many college classes, especially in such areas as political and sociological theory, and interdisciplinary fields like American Studies. The topic has formed the central question for adult discussion groups and Peace Corps training programs and is a fruitful adjunct to the study of nationalism and ideology. It is hoped that these articles will stimulate fresh definitions of democracy, especially in its American form, and provide some new clues to the specific strengths and weaknesses of our political culture.

I happily acknowledge the work of Professors Stuart Gerry Brown and Carol Ann Fisher, who initially used the question in their teaching when we served together on the Public Affairs faculty of the Maxwell Graduate School, Syracuse University. Different forms of this book were used by my students there, at the University of Southern California, and at Oregon State University.

E. G. M.

Corvallis, Oregon
October, 1967

(NOTE. — Throughout this book, the author-editor's footnotes are marked by symbols — *, † — and the original quoted notes by numerals.)

Contents

Introduction

After World War II, Americans were less innocently optimistic than the previous post-war generation had been about "making the world safe for democracy"; but we were still not well prepared to deal with the anti-democratic sentiments encouraged by years of all-out military organization. Strong nationalist movements erupted around the world, Western political leaders sometimes seemed to lose their firmness, and Americans were disturbed by the sudden spirit of intense rivalry with world communism.

We had entered World War II in a flurry of democratic rededication reminiscent of the Wilson days in 1917. Henry Luce, publisher of *Time* and *Life,* announced that "We are not in a war to defend American territory. We are in a war to defend and even promote, encourage and incite so-called democratic principles throughout the world." Combining technical assistance with free enterprise, Western democracy would transform itself. The American mission was clear:

> We must undertake how to be the Good Samaritan of the entire world. It is the manifest duty of this country to undertake to feed all the peoples of the world who as a result of this worldwide collapse of civilization are hungry and destitute — all of them, that is, whom we can from time to time reach consistently with a very tough attitude toward all hostile governments.*

Despite the great popularity of these views, manifested in the Four Freedoms of Roosevelt and Churchill, the Atlantic Charter, and our hopes for the United Nations, American democracy was a disappointing guide in the conduct of international relations. The decisions open to the United States might be met in several historically precedented alternative ways: (1) we could limit our concerns to our home territory and build a secure democracy as an example to the world; (2) we could encourage private enterprise to extend American ideas and practices overseas through economic expansion, supported by national policy; or (3) we could venture on an ideological crusade with the avowed aim of fostering democracy and

---

*Henry R. Luce, *The American Century* (New York: Farrar, 1941), pp. 10-14, 25, 36-37.

freedom in a free world.* The first policy, essentially isolationist, dominated American actions from the time of President Washington's Farewell Address, on through the formulation of the Monroe Doctrine, the Mexican War, the rush to the western frontier, our deadly Civil War, and up to our involvement in the Spanish-American War.

After our entry into that war in 1898, the second basic policy brought our participation in the imperialist expansion of the Western powers, and the nation took an active role in world affairs. American industry looked to new markets and new sources of raw materials. Senator Beveridge eloquently announced, "Our institutions will follow our flag on the wings of commerce."

American nationalism, and the attendant concepts of the nation's mission and destiny, assumed a new meaning; ideology was now explicitly allied with expansionist economic interests. Theodore Roosevelt and Admiral Mahan seriously conceived of a Pax Americana, despite the warnings of critics who decried the departure from the policies and ideals of the Founding Fathers. Other people's liberties were now to be protected by American sovereignty.

The third alternative policy involved Americans in World War I and carried us beyond outspoken economic and political self-interest into a moral crusade to guarantee democracy to all nations. But the nobility of the dream was matched by the thoroughness of its failure. Had we culpably failed to do justice to our promise, or was it simply that democracy could not be suited to all peoples? By 1920, after over a century of confused goals and means, we returned to our first choice, an isolationist policy that was in turn shattered twenty years later at Pearl Harbor.

In the assessment of our present relations with the world and the plotting of our future course, we are still faced with the essential question: Is American democracy exportable? The readings that follow comprise an intellectual journey in search of an answer. Do American ideals and institutions appear as sound when applied to foreign peoples and situations as they have in a strictly domestic context? What role have built-in cultural necessities played in our experience — in the arts and sciences, in religion and political philosophy, and in the intimate habits of daily life? When Americans deal with other people, do they start from American assump-

---

*See Hans J. Morgenthau, *The Purpose of American Politics* (New York: Knopf, 1960), pp. 99–114. I am completely indebted to him for his model of the three choices.

tions or from a knowledge of the people involved? Are our aid programs designed to encourage the democratic process, or only the outward forms of popular sovereignty and placid order?

These problems, and even the central question of democracy's exportability, are in turn only preliminary to any thorough appraisal of American foreign relations. For if it is decided that American political ideals are, indeed, susceptible to transplantation, there then arise the questions of whether it is desirable (and for whom) that they should be exported, and by what means this can best be accomplished. Do the three historical alternatives — isolation, economic expansion, ideological crusade backed by arms — exhaust the possibilities, or must we find a new path to follow in foreign affairs? Does our commitment to American democracy justify the use of military pressures to encourage its adoption elsewhere?

When the student has completed his reading and discussed the topic with others, he may still feel reluctant to give final answers to these crucial questions. But the problems demand answers, even if they are only tentative ones; history does not wait passively for our decisions. Perhaps, armed with a new sense of American purpose and power, interest and will, the reader will at least be prepared to consider new courses of action for his nation.

Chapter One

The American Democracy

Nations are not born democratic, not even America. It is unfortunately true that many Americans see the rest of the world only in terms of our national values; we cannot understand why others are so different from us and why they appear to want it that way. Some Americans, on the other hand, take the equally unfortunate attitude that ideals of government are really the same throughout the world — differences, they think, exist only because some people have progressed farther and see more clearly. The fact that both of these attitudes are reflected in the articles presented here testifies to the difficulty of our problem.

The Declaration of Independence and the Constitution — different documents written for quite different purposes — marked a spiritual starting point and laid down the political ground rules for the American system. The Declaration provided a metaphysical basis for our rights and liberties — equal for all men. Jefferson understood these as unalienable, self-evident moral axioms, not subject to proof. Today Americans accept them in the same unquestioning way. But our rights, however unalienable, have needed development by claims, tests, and reformulations. They are refined and qualified by our national experience. Can these same basic rights form the basis for a government that does not share the same history as ours? And are they, on the other hand, absolutely necessary for societies based on the democratic consent of the governed? To what extent are these rights essential to the development of a man's talent and a nation's energy? Because the Argentine Constitution is strikingly like ours, the study of that Republic with its dissimilar history is instructive. L. S. Rowe, however, warns us that appearances in this case are very deceiving.

As in so many areas of American life, there are two apparently conflicting forces embodied in our political system: individual liberty, and social order. These principles are frequently inconsistent with each other, yet they are generally accommodated peacefully. The tension is illuminated in Professor Brown's article, "American Democracy." In the next selection, three political scientists attempt to clarify the fundamentals upon which the democratic consensus is based. Do all Americans share this consensus? Research confirms that there is greater support for generalized, abstract democratic tenets than for the specifics of their application.* What is the meaning of consensus when we know that it is actually an active, influential minority which articulates our traditions, voices the public conscience, and watches over the health of our democracy?

Perhaps Americans have substituted for political realism a bright picture, an ideology, that flatters democracy and enlarges the importance of its principles. Other nations may be less interested in principles than in actions, but it is also true that ideals can guide behavior. Our study must begin with what we are as a conscientiously democratic nation and whether or not, because of what we are, we have something to offer others.

The Declaration of Independence (1776)

Thomas Jefferson

When in the Course of human events, it becomes necessary for one people to dissolve the political bands which have connected them with another, and to assume among the powers of the earth, the separate and equal station to which the Laws of Nature and of Nature's God entitle them, a decent respect to the opinions of mankind requires that they should declare the causes which impel them to the separation.

We hold these truths to be self-evident, that all men are created equal, that they are endowed by their Creator with certain unalienable Rights, that among these are Life, Liberty and the pursuit of Happiness. That to secure these rights, Governments are instituted

---

*For a revealing view, see Herbert McCloskey, "Consensus and Ideology in American Politics," *American Political Science Review*, LVIII (June, 1964); James Prothro and Charles Griggs, "Fundamental Principles of Democracy: Bases of Agreement and Disagreement," *Journal of Politics*, XXII (May, 1960); and V. O. Key, Jr., "Public Opinion and the Decay of Democracy," *Virginia Quarterly Review*, XXXVII (Autumn, 1961).

among Men, deriving their just powers from the consent of the governed. That whenever any Form of Government becomes destructive of these ends, it is the Right of the People to alter or to abolish it, and to institute new Government, laying its foundation on such principles and organizing its powers in such form, as to them shall seem most likely to effect their Safety and Happiness. Prudence, indeed, will dictate that Governments long established should not be changed for light and transient causes; and accordingly all experience hath shewn, that mankind are more disposed to suffer, while evils are sufferable, than to right themselves by abolishing the forms to which they are accustomed. But when a long train of abuses and usurpations, pursuing invariably the same Object evinces a design to reduce them under absolute Despotism, it is their right, it is their duty, to throw off such Government, and to provide new Guards for their future security.

. . . .

The Constitution of the United States (1787)

Preamble

We the People of the United States, in Order to form a more perfect Union, establish Justice, insure domestic Tranquility, provide for the common Defence, promote the general Welfare, and secure the Blessings of Liberty to ourselves and our Posterity, do ordain and establish this Constitution for the United States of America.

The Federal System of the Argentine Republic*

L. S. Rowe

Professor Rowe was a distinguished scholar on the faculty of Political Science at the University of Pennsylvania.

---

*From *The Federal System of the Argentine Republic* (Copyright 1921 by the Carnegie Institution of Washington), reprinted with permission.

Every commentator on the Argentine constitution has emphasized and in many cases exaggerated the influence of the Constitution of the United States upon the form and content of the Argentine federal system. In an opinion delivered on August 21, 1887, the supreme court of the Argentine Republic said:

> The system of government under which we are living was not of our creation. We found it in operation, tested by the experience of many years, and adopted it for our system. As has been well said, one of the great advantages of this plan has been that we were thus able to avail ourselves of the well-established rules of interpretation which serve as a guide in the application of the fundamental principles of the constitution in all those cases in which we have not altered the wording of the instrument.

Although the Constitution of the United States had exerted a far-reaching influence on Alberdi, whose work on the "bases of the Argentine Constitution" was used as a constitutional guide by the convention of 1853, the direct influence of the Constitution of the United States on the Argentine system is more clearly seen in the constitutional convention of the Province of Buenos Aires, convened in 1860 to propose amendments to the federal constitution. It was but natural that in this convention the spirit of states' rights should be more pronounced than in the national convention of 1853, and to support this position constant reference was made to the provisions of the Constitution of the United States.

The chairman of the committee on constitutional amendments of the Buenos Aires convention, in the report submitted to the convention, said:

> The federal form of government once accepted, the committee has been guided in its recommendations by the provisions of a similar constitution, recognized as the most perfect, viz., that of the United States.
>
> The provisions of this constitution are most readily applicable to Argentine conditions, having served as the basis for the formation of the Argentine Confederation.... The democratic government of the United States represents the last word of human logic, for the Constitution of the United States is the only one that has been made for and by the people.... It would, therefore, be both presumptuous and a proof of ignorance were we to attempt any innovations in con-

stitutional organization, thus ignoring the lessons of experience and the manifest truths accepted by human conscience.

In the convention of 1860, as in the convention of 1853, there was a marked tendency to exaggerate the influence of the form of government upon the destinies of the country. Thus the chairman of the committee on amendments to the constitution, Dr. Velez Sarsfield, in presenting the report of the committee, said:

> The Constitution of the United States has assured the happiness of a great continent for more than seventy years. The legislators of the Argentine adopted this constitution as their model . . . but did not respect its sacred text, and with ignorant hands attempted to improve upon it by suppressing certain provisions and by amending others. Your committee has done nothing more than restore to our system those portions of the constitutional law of the United States which the convention of 1853 attempted to modify.

It is also worthy of note that all the early commentators on the Argentine constitution were dominated by the principles formulated in the Constitution of the United States.

. . . .

In spite of the many points of similarity in the wording of the constitutions of Argentina and the United States, the constitutional practice of the two countries presents many contrasts of fundamental and far-reaching significance. The opportunity is thus afforded to study the operation of constitutional provisions identical in form under totally different conditions. Although the physical environment and economic conditions of the Argentine Republic present many points of similarity with certain regions of the United States, the political antecedents and traditions of the two countries are fundamentally different.

The establishment of a form of government in harmony with the dominant political ideas of the people does not constitute a guarantee that the subsequent development of the system or its actual operation will conform to the views of the founders of the system. The political ideals of a people may determine the establishment of a particular form of government, but its actual operation is determined by the forces beyond their control. It is this wide discrepancy between the views of the framers of the Argentine constitution and the actual operation of the political system that gives to its study so deep an interest to students of political science.

. . . .

American Democracy

Stuart Gerry Brown

This article was originally delivered as a speech (1964) at the Political Continuum at the University of Hawaii and was issued as an Occasional Paper in its Asia–America Program. It is reprinted by permission of the author, who is Professor of American Studies at the East–West Center of the University of Hawaii.

I

It may be useful at the outset to say something about what American democracy is *not*.

American democracy is not a system whose executive leader can be voted out of office by his cabinet, by the legislature, or by any small group of men and women acting on their own initiative and in their own interest. The American president may be denied a term of office only because a majority of the whole people believe it to be the national interest for him to be removed.

At this moment many thoughtful persons, in the United States and abroad, are congratulating the Soviet Union because it appears to have effected a peaceful transition from one executive to another. The Soviet Union is said to be maturing.

I do not patronize the Soviet Union when I express the hope that this is so. But it should not go unnoticed that of the two so-called super-powers which have been confronting each other now for almost twenty years, the one, the Soviet Union, has never consulted its people as to who shall be its leader, who shall make its laws, who shall determine its course of justice; while the other, the United States of America, has never failed to do so.

At the very moment that the Premier of the Soviet Union [Nikita Khrushchev] is being ousted in secret and in disgrace, the President of the United States is being challenged to defend his administration and his policy before the whole people, according to agreed upon rules, and in the certain knowledge that if he has won their confidence he will be returned to office, and that if he has not, his opponent will presently succeed him in a peaceable and orderly transfer of power.

The American democracy is not a system of government based upon any special doctrine of truth. It is not dedicated to proving either to itself or to the world that any one view of man and history is correct while others are mistaken. It is not dedicated to spreading either dogma or influence. It is, on the contrary, devoted only to protecting those who wish to govern themselves, and to spreading to the limits of the earth the "empire of liberty," which belongs to no man or nation because it belongs to every man and nation.

The American democracy is not a power structure which can be manipulated at will by one man, by a group of men, or by a political party. It is a plural system with many centers of power at many levels of life. Even its president, powerful as he is, is surrounded by limits upon his power imposed by law and by custom.

The American democracy is not a system in which the state has *abolished,* or claims to have abolished, the class struggle. It is, on the contrary, a system in which the people have *transcended* the class struggle by their rising scale of economic prosperity and their constant widening of the scope of access to power and leisure.

The American democracy is not a system in which the managers of industry determine public policy.

The American democracy is not a system in which the leaders of the trade unions determine public policy.

The American democracy, on the contrary, is a system in which the power of any one class is countervailed by the power of other classes. It is a system in which oppression and dictation are replaced by negotiation, collective bargaining, and compromise.

Thus, the American democracy is not a system in which everybody is happy and satisfied. It is, on the contrary, a society in which few individual persons, no group of persons, and no class of persons are ever satisfied with their *share* of wealth and power and prestige. But it is a system in which most persons, most groups, and all classes are satisfied with the *means of determining* what share they shall have.

That is why Justice William O. Douglas was right when he spoke of the American Communists as "miserable merchants of unwanted ideas." That is why no group or party which radically questions the means of determining public policy, of determining what share we shall have of the good things of life, has ever long succeeded in appealing to any large body of Americans.

It is for this reason, too, that American democracy is not based upon the clash of two sharply different ideological political parties. Despite the uncommonly sharp differences which divided the presidential candidates in the election of 1964—sometimes bordering on the ideological—even today the Republican and Democratic parties are more remarkable for what they have in common than for their differences.

They share the same premises as to the means of effecting change; they share the same belief in the efficacy of self-government; they share the same concern for individual liberty—social, economic, and religious. They share, in the end, the same vision of the United States as a land of equal opportunity resting both its economic and its moral hopes upon the people, not upon the government.

American democracy is not a system of unfettered freedom. No people and no system have ever set higher value upon individual liberty; but neither has any people or any system better understood that liberty must be inhibited by self-discipline and by social discipline if it is to be either a personal or a social reality.

It is the discipline of democracy which negatives the spontaneous impulses of men and of groups and of parties, when those impulses could not be expressed without frustration to the spontaneous impulses of other men or groups or parties.

Finally—to conclude this roundup of necessary negatives—the American democracy is not a panacea. It does not *solve* any of the great problems of individual life, of society, of international relations. It only *resolves* an issue, hangs on until the issue arises again, as it must, and then resolves it again.

American democracy endlessly temporizes, improvises, puts off—not because it lacks courage, but because it lacks certainty. And it lacks certainty because it accepts human beings as they are, not trying to mold them to some pattern held by theory or faith to be better.

As Mr. Madison put it long ago, "the seeds of faction are sown in the nature of man." Since this is so, there are only two ways to prevent their continuous eruption into violent social and political clashes. The one way is the way of suppression, tried and found wanting by all tyrannies from the beginning of time—wanting because tyranny can overcome factious conflict only by eliminating freedom. The other way is to negotiate and compromise and adjust, and then to negotiate, compromise, and adjust again, without end, because difference is without end so long as men are free to say what they think and do what they may do without harm to others. This is the way of the American democracy.

II

Let us turn now to some thoughts about what American democracy *is*.

American democracy is a system which allows a man to speak his piece no matter how hateful it may be, if he can find an audience to listen and if he does not incite to riot. . . .

American democracy allows anyone to state his case. But it does not allow him to conspire to teach or advocate the overthrow of the system by force or violence. American democracy does not recognize an obligation to serve its own destruction.

But American democracy is very patient. "It is time enough," said Mr. Jefferson, "for the rightful purposes of government, for its officers to interfere when principles break out into overt acts against peace and good order." Error of opinion, he said, is not to be feared "where reason is left free to combat it."

From time to time Americans have not practiced their democracy as diligently as they should have done, and holders of unpopular opinions have upon occasion been pilloried, and even jailed.

But the irrational moments of "Know–Nothingism," of Ku Klux Klanism, or of McCarthyism are in fact only moments. The American conscience is ashamed of them, and, as the *New York Times* said of the downfall of Senator McCarthy, the great majority are never infected, only lazy. In the end, and before it is too late, they "abate the thing" that betrays their faith in freedom, as they would abate any other public nuisance.

American democracy is a system in which a man accused of a crime can get a fair hearing and a fair trial.

In the American system an unsupported confession is not enough to convict. And confessions forced from the accused are not admissible as evidence. If there have been glaring exceptions, cases where justice and fairness have not prevailed, this is only to say that Americans are no less subject to error than are other peoples.

But American democracy is a system in which the minority who believe that the majority has committed an injustice, are not afraid to pursue their cause, indeed are free to pursue it indefinitely. Sacco and Vanzetti have been and are today both heroes and villains in American literature and law. Leon Trotsky is only a villain in the world of communism.

A Communist, or a Bircher, may be arrested, but he knows what law it is he is accused of violating, and he knows that the government goes into court with no privilege denied to him.

Indeed, it is a common criticism of American justice that it is too solicitous for the liberties of the accused. Policemen are hampered by law in their effort to enforce the law. Evidence revealing a man's guilt beyond any doubt may be disallowed because illegally obtained.

The American democracy is built upon the premise that to violate the civil liberty of one man is to jeopardize the civil liberties of all men.

American democracy announced its faith in human equality at the moment of the nation's birth. It has never succeeded in achieving full equality—but it has never ceased its effort.

The national tragic flaw was Negro chattel slavery. As the institution grew, so too did the opposition to it. The first anti-slavery men were Southern slaveholders. It was Mr. Jefferson who sought to bring an end to slavery in Virginia. All of the Founding Fathers shared his view. That they could not find a formula acceptable to enough people was, perhaps, their weakness.

But Jefferson's language was written into the Northwest Ordinance of 1787: "there shall be neither slavery nor involuntary servitude in the said territory." The Constitution contemplated the abolition of the international slave trade in 1808, and Mr. Jefferson had the honor of signing the bill that did so. Thereafter greed overtook idealism, and for fifty years the American conscience suffered, until it was purged in the Civil War.

There is no apology to be made for the American record in the matter of slavery. But it is fair to remind the critics of the United States that when the United States was conceived in liberty and dedicated to the proposition that all men are created equal, there was no other land as yet even making the attempt.

Discrimination followed the end of slavery, to the continued shame of American democracy. But the struggle for civil rights for Negroes was taken up by more and more Americans, until in the middle of the twentieth century it began to succeed.

The great American blight is at last disappearing—and rapidly. The revolutionary energy of the Negro people, aided by countless thousands of non-Negroes, and channelled for the most part into peaceful protest, has brought in 1964 a far-reaching Civil Rights Act to give force and life to our ideals. And Martin Luther King, a Negro leader of non-violent resistance, has won the Nobel Prize for Peace.

American democracy is a system in which many minorities have built a political process of claim and counter-claim. The people have come from every land and every race under the sun.

If each immigration has been jealous of the next, and much meanness has too often been practiced against the latest arrivals; if American laws have discriminated against peoples of the Orient because of prejudice and against people of southern Europe because of bigotry and condescension; if nativism has sometimes seemed like a national disease—American democracy has, nevertheless, accepted the oppressed and downtrodden of the world as no other country has ever done.

American minorities have built successful political organizations, elected full representation to city and state legislatures, and to the Congress of the United States.

In the Cabinet today sits a man of Italian extraction and another of Polish. On the Supreme Court have sat a succession of great Jewish justices. On the Court of Appeals there is a great Negro constitutional lawyer.* The Congressional delegation from this state includes two men of Japanese background, one of Chinese, and one of Northern European. And Boston, the original American city, founded by the Protestant saints of God to save one corner of the earth, so they believed, from the evils of popery, produced in the end an Irish Catholic president of the United States.

As E. B. White of the *New Yorker* once put it:

> The program, the dream, of the United States is in every respect great and inspiring, and we have nothing to hide and nothing to fear in that regard. But we must not fall into the error of the committee that recently elected the "prettiest schoolteacher in the United States" and published her name and photograph. The prettiest teacher in the United States is, we submit, a woman who runs into the tens of millions; she is the one locked in the heart of every scholar, young or old, who was ever in love with his teacher. And the prettiest program in the world does not bear the name and address of one country, one government, one philosopher, or one sect; it is the program that is held steadily in the hearts of all people: freedom, peace, justice, light, for all and the same for all. Our own country is merely best equipped to push it along, because of size and experience, and because we once put up a sign in the harbor saying "Send these, the homeless, tempest-tost to me . . . ," and because we meant it, and because they came.

American democracy brought freedom of conscience into being and has maintained it ever since.

The First Amendment to the Constitution; Mr. Jefferson's Virginia Statute for Religious Freedom; and a long line of decisions by the Supreme Court have underwritten religious liberty to the fullest extent ever known in the world.

When the United States came into being no nation had full religious freedom. The British practiced toleration, as had some of the American colonies before independence. But toleration presumes a body possessed of truth which will tolerate error. This was an advanced view in the eighteenth century, when most of the world's people were required not only to support a state church but to attend

*The references are to Louis Celebrezze, former Secretary of Health, Education, and Welfare and to John Gronouski, former Postmaster General and now Ambassador to Poland. Judge Thurgood Marshall, formerly of the Court of Appeals, and former Solicitor General of the United States, is now an Associate Justice of the United States Supreme Court.

it and profess its doctrines. As the American doctrine of the free conscience evolved, it maintained that since the reason of man is fallible, the truth cannot certainly be known. If it cannot certainly be known, there can be no body especially possessed of it. Without such a body toleration is irrelevant. And so the law in the United States came to be that "government shall make no law respecting an establishment of religion or prohibiting the free exercise thereof," and that no man may be required to profess a faith or compelled to worship in any way. No religious test may ever be required of a public official. Religion is left wholly to the conscience of the individual person.

In this system of total separation of church and state, the churches have flourished, as Mr. Madison predicted when he argued for freedom of conscience in 1786—at least as much as they have in countries where they are privileged by law.

To an American, Sunday is his day, to go to church, or to play golf, to go to the beach or to go to Sunday school—or to sit and study the baseball scores!

But whether Americans worship or not, they have learned that one man's orthodoxy may not be forced upon another, lest private conviction be submerged in public oppression.

American democracy is a system which permits unprecedented mobility.

And with mobility goes unprecedented opportunity. Horatio Alger was an American mythologist. But the people have always believed the myth no matter how cynically they have dismissed it. They have believed it because it is only an exaggeration of the truth that vertical mobility is encouraged by the American system. Progress in education, promotion in business or profession, are normal expectations.

And horizontal mobility has always been available for those who couldn't make it where they were. If the frontier was never quite the safety valve for the eastern unemployed that Frederick Jackson Turner supposed, it was nevertheless opened, and the west was settled by untold thousands of people seeking their fortunes.

Americans still seek their fortunes, confident that fortune-seeking is a natural right.

This is one of the reasons why socialism has never been attractive. *Security* is an American value, to be sure, and socialism appears to offer it; but *enterprise* is another American value, and socialism appears to smother it. The American system has been able to place a moving floor under its mobile population—or most of them—but there is no demand for a ceiling.

Last in this catalogue of things American democracy *is*, is the fact that it is supremely a *political* system. The political process, well or badly or indifferently conducted, is the characteristic process of American life.

Americans, unhappily, are deeply and inveterately prejudiced against "politicians." But they are nevertheless wholly dependent upon them. It is the process of politics, and the politicians who make it function, which preserves American liberty of opinion, of action, of protest.

The politician is suspect because he is a wheeler-dealer, because he is a compromiser. But it is precisely his wheeling and dealing, his compromising and negotiating that make it possible for the rest of us to be firm in our principles and unyielding in the rectitude of our opinions. *We* are happily right, so we think, while only the *politicians* are wrong!

The politician in the American democracy is the broker who negotiates the differences among free men and makes the system, if not efficient, at least viable—and our freedoms secure.

And it is politics which has enabled the American democracy to give the lie to the ingenious system of Karl Marx, to refute, indeed, not only communism but all other one-factor attempts to explain and predict the "inevitable" course of history.

Marx's fatal error was to assume that one factor—the economic—must determine everything else. Out of the class struggle between owner and worker, he taught, must come civil war, the final triumph of the worker, and a socialist society. So also taught Lenin and Stalin and Mao Tse-tung. The socialists agreed, except that they did not think civil war was necessary, since the workers might come to power through elections.

But the United Auto Workers, to take only the example of the moment, have just concluded negotiations with the auto managers which attest to the security of the workers, the profits of the companies, the improvement in the condition of both, and the absurdity of the class struggle doctrine.

What has happened is that politicians proved superior to economics.

Politicians, in their total function, reflect and work for a public interest greater than the interest of any class. They balance one force against another, taking direction neither from manager nor worker, though often from both, never satisfying either, but persuading both that the future may be theirs.

The politicians so regulated business in the interest of the nation that the age of monopoly became the age of reform. The politicians so interfered with the free market that depressions in the economy can never again be so severe as to shake the foundations of the system, as they did in 1929–1933.

The power of government is so vast that neither the power of business, nor of labor, nor of agriculture can hope to rival it. The government is, in the end, the representative of all three, as well as of the professions, the intellectuals, the old people, the children.

The American democracy is, above all, a system that thrives upon diversity. Racism and economic determinism, all absolutes and all dogmas, must be partial and tangential, if not merely hateful, to the majesty of a free people.

But if American democracy is sufficiently plural to contain an infinite variety of persons and places, ideas and beliefs, orthodoxies and heresies, it is also remarkably unified, and faces the world as one rather than many.

In a peculiar sense the American president is more representative of the nation and more the symbol of its democracy than the flag or the national anthem. Since we are in the midst of an election campaign, it may be fitting to celebrate today the president of the United States, whoever he is to be, as the sign of the American democracy. And I know of no better words than those of John Bright, an English statesman speaking of America a hundred years ago:

> ...to my mind there is nothing more worthy of reverence and obedience, and nothing more sacred, than the authority of the freely chosen magistrate of a great and free people; and if there be on earth and amongst men any right divine to govern, surely it rests with a ruler so chosen and so appointed.

Those words are as true today as they were a hundred years ago—they will still be true a hundred years in the future!

We Americans are a fortunate people—the most fortunate in all the history of mankind. In part, this is because we have been greatly endowed, as our forefathers would have said, by a kindly Providence, with natural riches which we have converted into wealth beyond the dreams of avarice. In part it is so because we unite in one polyglot people much of the best of all the races and religions and national traditions of the earth.

But in largest part, I am certain, it is because we have built a democratic way of life that better releases the creative thrust of the human spirit than does any other.

Our democracy is the oldest in the world—despite its youth. It has seen all the tyrannies of the modern world rise and fall—and fall they do and will, from Robespierre to Hitler and Stalin and the lesser tyrants of *this* day. It will survive *any* attack because, as John Kennedy said, Americans will make *any* sacrifice that may be needed to see that it does survive.

And American democracy will grow in light. This may not be the American century, as some have boastfully asserted; but if our achievements and our hopes are matched by humility it will continue to be a great century for Americans.

Cultural Prerequisites to a Successfully Functioning Democracy: A Symposium*

Ernest S. Griffith, John Plamenatz, J. Roland Pennock.

[*Ernest S. Griffith:*]

... "Democracy," whatever else may be included, implies free discussion and popular election of governors, with alternative choices

*Reprinted by permission of the authors and the publisher, the American Political Science Association, from *American Political Science Review,* L (March, 1956), 101–113, 119, 132.

Mr. Griffith is with the Library of Congress; Professors Plamenatz and Pennock are at Oxford University and Swarthmore College, respectively.

available. Presumably the governors will include a representative element, normally in the form of a legislative or policy-adopting body.

The term "cultural prerequisites" is less easily defined. The sociologists have an approach that sheds light upon that for which we are searching. They speak of the *mores,* those modes of thought as well as behavior by which men live and institutions are sustained. The *mores* are those elements of a culture which are regarded as essential for survival of the society itself. As regards democracy, our question is basically, "What is its cultural and psychological underpinning?" What cultural attitudes or *mores* will sustain democracy? In part they must do this by assuring its success in satisfying the psychological necessities of its citizens, in part by giving it and its institutions an emotional content which will make its survival a fighting matter for those who love it. Probing still more deeply, or moving, if you will, into another dimension, what will produce and sustain these attitudes? Is there, by chance, a central matrix of which they are derivatives?

Conversely, can the necessity of these attitudes be demonstrated by proving the probability of failure if they are absent?

. . . .

. . . We have chosen to exclude any detailed discussion of political institutions as such, in part because these have so frequently been the subject of scholars' concern. We are united in asserting the importance and relevance to democracy and its flourishing survival of such institutions as the single-member constituency, constitutional responsibility, local self-government, the two-party system, a career civil service. Yet are not these more in the nature of by-products or derivatives of the attitudes which we regard as cultural prerequisites than themselves basic?

. . . Belief in democratic institutions may well be a cultural prerequisite to their survival; but such a belief must take the form of a fighting and deep conviction, which itself may well be a product of attitudes still more basic.

That there be no misunderstanding, it will not be enough for any of us to say that education is an answer. We are still left with the question: "What education?" In other words, what attitudes would we create, identify, intensify, transmit, motivate, make instruments of demonstrated satisfaction, in the educational process itself?

We shall delimit our problem by confining our attention to democracy in the large, modern, industrialized state.

We concede that democracy is more likely to survive, other things being equal, in small states. Such states are more manageable, in that the results of specific political action are more readily identifiable. Advantages and disadvantages are more clearly demonstrable. And there are other favorable circumstances which need not detain us here.

An agrarian state of small landowners is likely to present fewer difficulties. This combines the advantages of diffusion of property with economic homogeneity.*

A state unthreatened by external enemies probably finds it relatively easy to develop and sustain democratic institutions, even though the latter may command a loyalty of relatively low temperature.

A state the tempo of whose social change is slow and devoid of stress and strain would seem to pose less of a problem in maintenance of its democratic institutions.

In the foregoing statements we freely concede the presence of a number of variables besetting our problem. While these variables are to a degree independent of the attitudes for which we are searching, they do affect measurably the necessity or otherwise of a strong psychological underpinning as regards democratic survival.

. . . .

. . . It is my hypothesis that the Christian and Hebrew faiths constitute a powerful matrix, a common denominator of those attitudes most essential to a flourishing democracy. Moreover, it would appear that it is these faiths, and especially the Christian faith, that perhaps alone can cloak such attitudes with the character of "absolutes" —a character which is not only desirable, but perhaps even necessary to democratic survival.

. . . .

Let us now consider affirmatively each attitude of the series I propose as prerequisites. . . .

It is not accidental that I give first place to the value placed upon individual personality, or rather the view of the nature of the indi-

*For a contrary view, see Roscoe C. Martin, *Grass Roots* (University, Ala.: University of Alabama Press, 1957).

vidual as being end and not means. The heart of freedom as a hallmark of democracy consists in a formal or informal constitutional allocation to the individual of certain areas of action which no government (or for that matter, no social institution, including business and labor organizations) may touch. Montesquieu's age called these areas "natural rights"—freedom of speech, freedom of worship, freedom from arbitrary or lawless acts. Jefferson spoke of the inalienable rights of "life, liberty, and the pursuit of happiness," and gave them a theological grounding. . . .

As political scientists, we may at least observe the effect on attitude of regarding a man—any man—as a child of God. It provides a norm by which political and economic conduct is to be judged. There are things, if you will, which one who regards himself as a child of God just does not do to another child of God. One does not exploit him, for example; nor does one terrorize or cheat or deceive him; nor irrationally and arbitrarily coerce him. Conversely and affirmatively it leads straight to a conviction of the importance of justice for the individual. It also defines justice by providing norms.

It may not be enough to think of liberty or freedom merely as useful culture traits, to be adopted or discarded according to whether or not what appears to be a still more useful trait—security or national survival, for example—is advanced as preferable but incompatible. For democracy to survive in the large, complex, insecure industrialized state, it may well be essential that its participants shall love liberty—for others as well as for themselves—with a passion that finds it more precious than life. I raise the question as to whether anything less than a theological base is adequate upon which to build a society of the free.

In the second place, a democracy withers away if its people lose interest in its institutions and their constructive use for the general welfare. This is a much wider matter than merely voting or not voting, though this latter is certainly a relevant barometer. Its importance extends to every form of responsible citizen participation in community life: to business and industry, social work, religious activity, as well as to formal government. In government it also means alertness, and the communication of alertness, between elections. Willingness to accept or even to seek office must be sufficiently widespread among the civic minded to assure a measure of disinterested service. Careers in public administration must have attached to them a prestige and an appeal equal to those of other professions.

If such wide participation is lacking, or (if present) is largely self-centered, then greed, graft, negativism, materialism, sensualism will quickly erode the quality of civic life. A nation will become a nation of cynics.

. . . .

I am speaking here of the need for responsible participation. By this I mean an affirmative attitude toward society, an attitude that places obligations at least on a par with rights; that in blunt and governmental terms expects to pay taxes in return for services; that in larger terms accepts and welcomes the opportunity to expend effort in behalf of the general welfare or the good of all.

. . . .

There is a third motive or principle necessary to sustain democracy. All definitions of democracy have at least this in common: they agree that discussion preceding decision (and, for that matter, free and critical discussion following a decision) is one of its major attributes. If such a discussion is to be full and free, if ideas are to win their way in the market place of reason, then characteristic institutions such as a free press, free communications, open sessions of parliaments and chambers and congresses, judicial processes allowing a man his "day in court" are corollaries. New institutions may be needed, better devised to bring technical competence to bear upon decisions or better able to clarify issues. But these are not primary.

. . . .

The fourth prerequisite for a successfully functioning democracy carries one into the economic order.

We all know that the industrial age has brought with it specialization, and that this specialization has divided men into various economic groups—labor, industry, finance, the professions, agriculture, and others—and that these great groups are subdivided, sometimes sharply so, into all sorts of sub-groups: coal miners, bankers, physicians, dairy farmers, steel manufacturers, and literally thousands of others. These form the warp and woof of our economic life. We appreciate the extent to which they likewise characterize and at times dominate our political life as well. Each of these groups more or less lives in its own limited world; its members experience the same frustrations, enjoy the same advantages, and thus have come to a considerable extent to share the same political point of view, which in turn diverges to a greater or less extent from that held by other groups. In the United States these divergent points of view of this multitude of economic groups are the greatest single phenomenon in what we call politics and public opinion.

. . . .

In the fifth place, the office holder, be he elected or appointed, occupies a key place in contemporary society. Leadership seems destined to be more and more concentrated. As life baffles more and more of us, there is an almost inevitable tendency to seek for and to follow the man who gives us the impression of adequacy. Such may be the demagogue whose noises coincide with our own prejudices. Such may also be the elected leader of character who moves surely, strongly, among the manifold problems and pitfalls of a world in disorder. Then, too, the sphere of government is enormously extended. This is true, not only of overt state action, but even more of the far wider sphere in which governmental decisions affect or influence in what is technically the sector of private industry or spontaneous social behavior.

Moreover, the "mysteries" of technology and specialization multiply the opportunities of the office holder unobserved to behave irresponsibly through inertia, self-seeking, and undetected error.

Hunger for power, carelessness, self-seeking, intrigue, corruption—these hold dangers for our democracies, if once they come to characterize our men in public life. In the more simple days—of, shall we say, Restoration England or the period of Boss Tweed or the Grant administration in the United States—betrayals of public trust more crass and despicable in themselves than those of today did not have the far-reaching consequences which today follow a lowering of the tone of public life.

. . . .

A final prerequisite for the present atomic age is an attitude toward humanity that transcends nationalism. It will not have to be argued with the vast majority of readers that the old loyalties of the nineteenth century are inadequate to the mid-twentieth century. The indivisibility of at least the free world is axiomatic, if for no other reason than its sharing of a common menace. It is not beyond the bounds of reason to say that the time may be not too far distant in which the free world and the iron curtain world may both see an uncontrolled science as their common enemy, an enemy so awful as to threaten both alike with destruction. In such a setting a widespread, deeply felt belief in world brotherhood may well be required, especially in the free world. Our greater strength may tempt us to forget our common humanity with the enslaved and deluded millions allegedly our enemies. Moreover, out from the more developed peoples of the free world there must flow to the underdeveloped peoples of other races and continents assistance in their self-emancipation from ignorance, disease, poverty, colonialism, exploitation, race discrimination, terror. Some of this help will continue to be through missionaries. Some will be through industry, capital and labor alike. More and more such aid is apparently destined to be governmental. This I take it is the meaning of the Technical Assistance Program under the United Nations, the Colombo Plan, the Point IV Program.

. . . .

We have too often been content to treat the forms of government as being the heart of government. We have not looked to the substance. When we do look to the substance we find that the motives of men hold the key. I take it that the overwhelming majority of the readers subscribe to the democratic way. Do we see the price to be paid for its survival, over and above military strength or economic health? I submit the following as the necessary attitudes to sustain democratic institutions:

1. Love for and belief in freedom: best based upon belief in the sacredness of the individual as a child of God.

2. Active and constructive participation in community life: best based upon the obligation of the Christian, the Jew, and other believers to accept responsibilities, cooperating with and working for their brother men.

3. Integrity in discussion: best based upon the inner light of truth being primary in a world God meant to be righteous.

4. The freely assumed obligation of economic groups to serve society; best based upon the Christian insight into the nature of society as set forth, for example, by the parable of the body and its members.

5. Leadership and office holding regarded as public trusts: best based upon or inspired by the example and teachings of religious prophets, such as Jesus, who accepted such a service "to the death."

6. Attitudes assuring that passion will be channeled into constructive ends: best based upon religious faiths that unite an obligation to love and serve with a recognition of the primacy of individual personality.

7. Friendliness and cooperation among nations: best based upon the vision of world brotherhood derived from a faith that we are all children of a common Heavenly Father.

I freely grant that many of these attitudes would be helpful also to non-democratic forms of government, especially the fifth. I seriously doubt, however, that at least the basis of any of them could have anything but the most precarious existence except in a democracy.

. . . .

[*John Plamenatz:*]

After respect for personal rights, for privacy and independence, I should put, as a cultural prerequisite of democracy, respect for law, for judicial and political processes, not for their own sake, but as means to security and freedom. This, too, is something to be defined more particularly if it is to be shown how exactly it is a condition of democracy. I do not speak of respect for law merely as such. For that kind of respect has existed in many societies that were not democratic. What I speak of is the respect for law resulting from the love of freedom; it is a respect for the judicial and political processes which, in a large and intricate society, are known to be conditions of freedom. These processes are elaborate and difficult to describe. . . . These processes preserve order and protect liberty, and yet do not prevent change. They make change easy and acceptable provided it is carried out according to definite rules.

. . . .

[*J. Roland Pennock:*]

One of the most important and distinctive elements of the democratic ethic, one certainly deserving of listing as a prerequisite, is an attitude of tolerance for difference, of willingness to compromise. . . . Closely related to the willingness to compromise, is respect for rules and set procedures. Not only the basic rule of decision by majorities but also innumerable rules and understandings as to procedure are fundamental to successful operation of the democratic process. The American congressional system is completely dependent, for instance, on such understandings as that the majority party will allow adequate minority representation on committees and that the minority representatives will be allowed opportunities for effective participation. Only when participants in a democratic organization of any kind feel assured that the rules will be adhered to are they likely to accept willingly decisions that affect their interests adversely. Democracy is like a game: unless the participants adhere to the rules it fails of its purpose and will soon break down completely.

. . . .

While I would stress the importance of an "economic margin" for the development of attitudes favorable to democracy—and especially I would urge the disqualifying effects of extreme poverty—it would be far from my point to urge any one-to-one correlation between prosperity and democracy. It is even possible that too much prosperity may be unfavorable to democratic attitudes. What I am contending is that "conditioned humanitarianism" grows naturally out of a situation where individuals have time and opportunity for forming free and relatively permanent associations in many types of groups, ranging from the family up. Some will be professional and vocational, others will be of the "service" variety. Some will have neighborhood or other geographical bases, while many will unite individuals from different areas. . . .*

---

*Compare these prerequisites with the commentaries of McCloskey, *op. cit.*; Prothro and Griggs, *op. cit.*; Seymour Martin Lipset, "Some Social Requisites of Democracy: Economic Development and Political Legitimacy," *American Political Science Review*, LIII (March, 1959); Daniel Lerner, *The Passing of Traditional Society* (New York: The Free Press, 1958), pp. 49–52, 60–62; Gabriel Almond and Sidney Verba, *The Civic Culture* (Princeton: Princeton University Press, 1963), pp. 11–32, *passim*; 492.

Chapter Two

The American Democracy as Experience for Revolutionary Nationalism

Can we posit an ideal American man, defined by our national heritage? Has our nation produced the archetypical modern man, towards whom all men are moving? In his *Letters from an American Farmer* (1782), de Crevecoeur asserted that "Americans are the western pilgrims," and suggested that they "act upon 'new principles' and form new opinions." Frederick Jackson Turner believed the unique American character was best explained by the experience of pioneering the Western frontier. But in the middle of the twentieth century, without a land frontier to exploit, the space frontier may not be an effective substitute. Do the qualities of character developed in civilizing the West apply easily to the demands of science, industry, and technology in modern society?

Professor Potter maintains that the growth of our material wealth has not been dependent on our political system. Abundance has shaped our democracy, not democracy our abundance. Not understanding this relationship, Americans have misinterpreted developments in other nations. In a time when the gap between rich and poor widens, both within and between nations, it is a serious mistake to resent the failure of economically underdeveloped countries to embrace our ideals, when in fact our ideals make sense only when supported by economic affluence.

Professors Degler and Boorstin believe that our own historical experience and political principles are poor equipment for understanding the rest of the world. And since it is not doctrine or theory but our unique circumstances that are responsible for the shape of American success, it is made that much more difficult to apply our standards to the problems of foreign nations. Our example is inapplicable to the situations of most others. According to Lucius Beebe, our technology is nevertheless much more attractive and understandable to the rest of the world than our ideology. He suggests that high ideals will be most effectively promoted by building tall hotels abroad.

Thus, however successful our doctrine and our economic system have been for us, Americans cannot rest on their laurels. It may be that we must reconstruct our revolutionary ideals to compete with rival ideologies in the interest of simple self-preservation. Ralph Waldo Emerson, writing a century ago, believed that "Americans have a disposition to trust a principle more than a material force." Is this still true?

Letters from an American Farmer (1782)

J. Hector St. John de Crèvecoeur

Often referred to as the second greatest literary work of the colonial period, after Franklin's *Autobiography,* is Michael (J. Hector St. John) de Crevecoeur's account of his life and journeys in the colonies and the states from the time he served in the French armies in New France, through their defeat, to his naturalization and residency as an American. He has a sharp faculty for seeing the ideal and the achievement of his adopted land.

. . . What then is the American, this new man? He is either an European, or the descendant of an European, hence that strange mixture of blood, which you will find in no other country. I could point out to you a family whose grandfather was an Englishman, whose wife was Dutch, whose son married a French woman, and whose present four sons now have four wives of different nations. He is an American, who, leaving behind him all his ancient prejudices and manners, receives new ones from the new mode of life he has embraced, the new government he obeys, and the new rank he holds. He becomes an American by being received in the broad lap of our great Alma Mater. Here individuals of all nations are melted into a new race of men, whose labours and posterity will one day cause great changes in the world. Americans are the western pilgrims, who are carrying along with them that great mass of arts, sciences, vigour, and industry which began long since in the east; they will finish the great circle. The Americans were once scattered all over Europe; here they are incorporated into one of the finest systems of population which has ever appeared, and which will hereafter become distinct by the power of the different climates they inhabit. The American ought therefore to love this country much better than that wherein either he or his forefathers were born. Here the rewards of his industry follow with equal steps the progress of his labour; his labour is founded on the basis of nature, self-interest; can it want a stronger allurement? Wives and children, who before in vain demanded of him a morsel of bread, now, fat and frolicsome, gladly help their father to clear those fields whence exuberant crops are to arise to feed and to clothe them all; without any part being claimed, either by a despotic prince, a rich abbot, or a mighty lord. Here religion demands but little of him; a small voluntary salary to the minister, and gratitude to God; can he refuse these? The American is a new man, who acts upon new principles; he must therefore entertain new ideas, and form new opinions. From involuntary idleness, servile dependence, penury, and useless labour, he has passed to toils of a very different nature, rewarded by ample subsistence.—*This in an American.*

The Significance of the Frontier in American History (1920)*

Frederick Jackson Turner

Turner's Frontier Thesis of the origins and uniqueness of the American democratic tradition is perhaps the single most seminal and controversial in a long history of explanations. Professor Turner served brilliantly on the History faculties at the University of Wisconsin and later at Harvard University. He originally announced his thesis in an address before the American Historical Association in 1893, when he was thirty-two years old and had only recently completed graduate school.

...Up to our own day American history has been in a large degree the history of the colonization of the Great West. The existence of an area of free land, its continuous recession, and the

*From *The Frontier in American History* by Frederick Jackson Turner, copyright 1920 by Frederick J. Turner, copyright 1948 by Caroline M. S. Turner. Reprinted by permission of Holt, Rinehart and Winston, Inc.

advance of American settlement westward, explain American development. . . .

But the most important effect of the frontier has been in the promotion of democracy here and in Europe. As has been indicated, the frontier is productive of individualism. Complex society is precipitated by the wilderness into a kind of primitive organization based on the family. The tendency is anti-social. It produces antipathy to control. The tax-gatherer is viewed as a representative of oppression. Prof. Osgood, in an able article, has pointed out that the frontier conditions prevalent in the colonies are important factors in the explanation of the American Revolution, where individual liberty was sometimes confused with absence of all effective government. The same conditions aid in explaining the difficulty of instituting a strong government in the period of the confederacy. The frontier individualism has from the beginning promoted democracy. . . .

From the conditions of frontier life came intellectual traits of profound importance. The works of travelers along each frontier from colonial days onward describe certain common traits, and these traits have, while softening down, still persisted as survivals in the place of their origin, even when a higher social organization succeeded. The result is that to the frontier the American intellect owes its striking characteristics. That coarseness and strength combined with acuteness and inquisitiveness; that practical, inventive turn of mind, quick to find expedients; that masterful grasp of material things, lacking in the artistic but powerful to effect great ends; that restless, nervous energy; that dominant individualism, working for good and for evil, and withal that buoyancy and exuberance which comes with freedom—these are traits of the frontier, or traits called out elsewhere because of the existence of the frontier. Since the days when the fleet of Columbus sailed into the waters of the New World, America has been another name for opportunity, and the people of the United States have taken their tone from the incessant expansion which has not only been open but has even been forced upon them. He would be a rash prophet who should assert that the expansive character of American life has now entirely ceased. Movement has been its dominant fact, and, unless this training has no effect upon a people, the American energy will continually demand a wider field for its exercise. . . .

People of Plenty*

David M. Potter

Economic abundance has shaped the distinctive democratic character of the American people. Americans are mistaken in their belief that freedom and abundance necessarily converge in any meaningful way for other peoples. Professor Potter served many years as Coe Professor of American History at Yale University, chairman of its American Studies program, and editor of the *Yale Review* before his appointment as Professor and Executive Head of the Department of History at Stanford University.

The thought is not original with me, but what I would suggest is this: that we have been historically correct in supposing that we had a revolutionary message to offer but we have been mistaken in our concept of what that message was. We supposed that our revelation was "democracy revolutionizing the world," but in reality it was "abundance revolutionizing the world"—a message which we did not preach and scarcely understood ourselves, but one which was peculiarly able to preach its own gospel without words. . . .

For a country destined, as ours has been, to play such a role it was a tragic fallacy that we conceived of democracy as an absolute value, largely ideological in content and equally valid in any environment, instead of recognizing that our own democratic system is one of the major by-products of our abundance, workable primarily because of the measure of our abundance. . . . I have already attempted to discuss this point in a context of domestic affairs and to show our error in thinking of democracy as a system which we have because, out of our superior political wisdom and virtue, we chose it, when, in fact, any credit that we give to ourselves ought to be for creating the conditions that would enable it to work and would enable us to afford it. On the domestic scene, the fallacy was more or less academic in its

*From Chapter VI, "Abundance and the Mission of America," in David M. Potter, *People of Plenty* (Chicago, 1954).

consequences, which is perhaps why we have been slow to perceive it. The only adverse result was to bring us to the right operative conclusions for the wrong reasons.

But on the international front this fallacy has had most far-reaching results, in that it has consistently impelled us to proselyte for converts to the democratic faith in places where the economic prerequisites for democracy have not been established. This, I believe, has a great deal to do with the widespread impression in the world that the Americans are, somehow, hypocrites. In our own country the promise of equality meant the right to advance, without discrimination, to easily attainable ends. Hence the principle of equality could be upheld with genuine sincerity. Freedom meant the removal of barriers to advancement from one position to another, more advantageous one. But in countries where even decency, much less comfort, lay beyond the point of attainability for most people—where the number of advantageous positions was negligible—it seemed a kind of deception to offer the individual as good a chance as anyone to compete for nonexistent prizes or to assure him of his freedom to go where he wished, when there was, in fact, nowhere to go.

This anomalous relationship between the permissive and the protective aspects of freedom has always required adjustment, both at the domestic and at the international level. Thus Franklin Roosevelt, who, on the domestic front, shifted the emphasis from freedom as immunity to control, to freedom as immunity to social privation, also recognized the need for giving new connotations to the term "freedom" on the international scene. Hence his four freedoms—freedom of speech, freedom of religion, freedom from want, and freedom from fear—were two parts freedom in the classic liberal sense and two parts security under the label of "freedom."

If Roosevelt had been able to fulfill his formula, the whole nature of this problem would be different; but he was not, and we revert to the fact that American liberals throughout our history have misunderstood the nature of our own economic revolution and have also misunderstood what the revolutionists of other countries wanted. Jefferson and his landowning, independent, backwoods farmers, who had conducted a political revolution against Britain without social upheaval, were not prepared for the convulsions that an oppressed class of serfs and a Paris mob would regard as a necessary part of any reform that was worth making in France. Henry Clay and the expansive westerners did not appreciate that in Latin America, behind the few idealists who believed in liberty, there was a local ruling class which saw no reason why absentees in Europe should continue to share in the exploitation of the Indians and who proposed to monopolize this exploitation for themselves. The idealists who felt it a national obligation to liberate Cuba in 1898 did not appreciate that the Cubans were revolting against economic conditions which resulted even more from the McKinley Tariff than from the iniquities of Bourbon misrule. American liberals in 1919 and 1920 failed to grasp the fact that Russian revolutionaries were overthrowing the ruthless regime of the tsars not because they wanted to substitute a more humanitarian regime in its place but because they wanted to substitute a more efficient ruthlessness, and one which would be operated by a different class.

The most effective means by which we could have promoted humanitarian and democratic principles abroad was not by applauding revolutions conducted in the name of such principles but by imparting to other parts of the world the means that we have developed for raising the standard of living. On the face of it, this assertion may seem inconsistent with the whole thesis of these chapters, namely, that the United States enjoyed a richer endowment than other countries and that this physical heritage has influenced our past history and our present society in distinctive ways. But no less important than the original, easily accessible wealth was the fact that this wealth stimulated our technology and our entire productive system in such a way that we developed an unparalleled aptitude for converting many previously inconvertible materials and sources of power into forms that also constituted wealth. If we were unique in the original heritage, we are not at all unique in the possession of potential assets whose value may be realized by the application of technological skill. Thus we are in position to affirm to the world that, although we are in many respects set apart by our natural plenty, in many other respects we are qualified to show other countries the path that may lead them to a plenty like our own. But we have thrown away this opportunity by failing to display the processes which others might emulate and by showing, instead, the end-product—our standard of living—which they can only envy. Then we have deepened the alienation by blaming other peoples for failing to embrace the political ideals which our standard of living supports.

In spite of the early export of such American technological devices as the McCormick reaper and in spite of attempts, through the Point Four program, to stimulate production in undeveloped countries, it remains painfully true that we have urged other nations to adopt our democracy as their own, while encouraging them to draw upon our abundance in such a way (by the importation of consumer goods) that it remains distinctively our own. Democracy has been held up as a matter of political morality, involving privileges of citizenship which mean little to people below a certain economic level, and it has not been presented as a highly flexible social system conducive to the economic energy and growth which provide abundance. Abundance has been presented as an entirely separate feature of American life and has been manifested to the world primarily in the form of consumer goods which excite the international envy of those whose needs they satisfy, without in any way removing either the sources of envy or the sources of need. Consequently, America's abundance has probably done more to cut us off from actual moral leadership than it has done to enhance such leadership. And certainly it has placed American generosity—much of which is both genuine and unselfish—under the curse of chronic envy.

As a result, our message to the world has become involved in a dilemma: to other peoples, our democracy has seemed attainable but not especially desirable; our abundance has seemed infinitely desirable but quite unattainable. But, if the realities of the relationship between democracy and abundance had been understood by people of other countries or, what is more to the point, by those Americans who were seeking to impart our message, our democracy would have seemed more desirable, and our abundance would have seemed more attainable. Both these changes would have had the effect of strengthening the moral influence of the United States.

In this brief consideration of a tremendously complex subject which has challenged all the skill of large staffs of trained workers in our government, there is no intention to imply that a simple and easy solution for international difficulties lies ready at hand. Nor would I suggest that these workers have universally lacked insight into the relationship between democracy and abundance. But, in so far as they may have possessed such insight, certainly they must have been hindered by the general lack of understanding of this matter both at home and abroad. We have talked so much about "free enterprise" as if we just meant laissez faire economics (which all too often is what we did mean) and so much about "democracy" as if we meant some vague, yearning fraternalism (which, again, is too often what we did mean) that we have failed to make the point that democracy paced the growth of our abundance and abundance broadened the base of our democracy.

Thus our whole conception of our mission in the world was distorted by our failure to understand what the world regarded as most significant in our development and what the essential conditions of democratic life in the American sense really are. The factor of abundance, which we first discovered as an environmental condition and which we then converted by technological change into a cultural as well as a physical force, has not only influenced all the aspects of American life in a fundamental way but has also impinged upon our relations with the peoples of the world, and our failure to realize the nature of the relationship between this abundance and our democracy has played a critical part in frustrating our attempts to fulfill the mission of America.

Revolutionary Nationalism*

Carl N. Degler

The author is a distinguished professor of American history at Vassar College.

Is American History a Usable Precedent?

Increasingly, it is fashionable to discern a connection between our own successful revolt against colonial rule and the revolt against Europe that is the essence of the nationalist ferment in Asia and

*Originally published as "The American Past: An Unsuspected Obstacle in Foreign Affairs," *The American Scholar*, XXXII (Spring, 1963), and copyrighted, 1963, by the United Chapters of Phi Beta Kappa, this article appears here by permission of the author and publishers exactly as it was abridged and reprinted in *Current* (July, 1963), 28–31.

Africa. . . . But a closer inspection of the American past suggests that our experience is too special to be a guide to the life of other people; to suppose that what we did can be done by others simply because we did it, is to misread our history and, more important, to confuse our people and to misunderstand what is going on in the underdeveloped world.

Take the example of our colonial revolution from Great Britain. On the surface it is a simple war for independence against the greatest power of the day. Viewed as such it appears strikingly similar to the Indian movement for independence or the Indonesian revolt against the Dutch. But once we probe beneath the surface the analogy quickly evaporates.

A salient feature of our revolution was that its animating purpose was deeply conservative. The colonials revolted against British rule in order to keep things as they were, not to initiate a new era. . . . The demand for independence came only reluctantly and after years of trial and agitation and when the imperial purpose of the British seemed incapable of being turned aside in any other fashion. . . .

Independence became a goal for Americans only as a "dernier resort," as Washington was fond of saying. The men who pushed the American Revolution were not nationalists compelled to spend years in the jails of the colonial power, but political leaders seeking only to continue their free governments as they knew them all their lives. Fully three-quarters of the men who signed the Declaration of Independence held office under the Crown before the Revolution and under the state governments immediately after the Revolution. What other colonial country today can show a similar degree of continuity of leadership across the chasm of its revolution for independence?

More is at stake here than simple historical accuracy. Our whole conception of what a revolution is and how independence is achieved has been shaped by our historical experience. It is true, of course, as has been pointed out by a number of commentators, that as a result of their own successful revolt Americans in the eighteenth, nineteenth and twentieth centuries were prone to welcome revolutions elsewhere. But the significant fact is that when these revolutions did not emulate the American pattern of quickly leading to orderly, democratic societies, American public opinion found these foreign revolutions disappointing. . . .

Another analogy often made between the history of the United States and the newly emergent nations is that America began as an underdeveloped country, successfully making the transition to industrialization without government controls or interference with individual initiative. Therefore, it is argued, if Americans could do it in the past, then these new nations can today. Why, then, many Americans today ask in rising anger, do these nations need foreign aid, why do they lean so sympathetically toward socialistic measures and state intervention in economic affairs?

Again the answer must be that the analogy is wrong. It is true that in the early years of the Republic the United States was largely agrarian in economy, deceptively similar in character to those traditional societies now emerging into statehood. But the United States was an agricultural society in which the ratio between man and land was low. "Here everyone may have land to labor for himself," Jefferson pointed out in 1813. Sometimes the land speculator made the acquisition of land more difficult or more expensive than might otherwise have been the case, but as early as 1820, an eighty-acre piece of land could be purchased from the government for one hundred dollars. In a nation where most men were landowners, few Americans had to contend with landlords or moneylenders, as has been the case with Indians crowded upon their tiny plots in Bengal and the Oudh. And when they did, as in New York state in the 1830's and 1840's, the force of the rest of society supported the overthrow of feudal encumbrances. . . .

An American in the early nineteenth century, as a result of his own hard labor, could accumulate a surplus, even buy more land (and, if he lived in the South, more slaves) and greatly improve his material position in his own lifetime. The thirty-eight million immigrants who entered the United States between 1820 and 1930 were living testimony to the belief in and the actuality of the opportunity. The immigrants came also because wages were high in the United States, for in the new country there was a chronic, if variable, shortage of labor. High wages in turn encouraged a rising rate of productivity through the use of machines and labor-saving devices on farms and in factories. (Even slave labor was too expensive at times and so Yankee ingenuity and Southern profit-seeking combined to produce a cotton gin.) In the new nations of the world, the two great problems that inhibit economic growth are low agricultural productivity and a high ratio of men to land. America in its rise to economic abundance has not had to contend with such difficult obstacles.

One can carry the story further into the era of industry. As agricultural productivity rose, more men could be spared from farming to serve in the industrial labor force in the expanding cities. The very prosperity of the countryside meant that an internal market for manufactures was already in being. Furthermore, the generally high wage rates in the cities—as compared with contemporary Europe, to say nothing of Asia, Africa and South America today—provided a still better and wider market for manufactures in the urban centers by the close of the century. Obviously the story of the American transition from agriculture to industry is more complex than can be described here, but it is evident that the circumstances that brought that transition about are largely absent from the underdeveloped countries of the world today.

There is further reason why the economic growth of the United States offers few analogies for the new nation. One of the consequences of the abundance of natural resources was that the nation could afford to leave economic activity up to individual initiative, with all that that meant in offering a powerful incentive to production. A less well-endowed society could not have afforded to give free rein to the individual, for, as is evident in American history, individual enterprise is often rather free and easy in its use of national resources. Waste, contrary to Vance Packard, is not an invention of modern Americans. From the very beginning of our history foreign travelers have commented upon the slovenly agriculture of Americans. . . . Such a casual approach to national wealth and the labor force is not possible in a nation in which resources are limited—or already partly exhausted by the colonial power—and the pressure of population upon the land is already intense. . . .

With so many nations turning to socialism or planning, Americans find their own history a poor guide to the world. Historically, socialism is the doctrine of the working class in an industrial society. But the irony of history is that the United States, as the most thoroughly industrialized country on the globe, has never experienced a socialist movement. The reasons are too lengthy to go into here; the important point is that socialism is an alien and unfamiliar phenomenon to most Americans. At best it seems an unnecessary interference with liberty of enterprise and a violation of the proper role of the state as our history has defined that role for us. Even in the days of the New Deal and the modern welfare state, the idea that the government should own enterprises and be an employer of industrial labor on a large scale has had no basis either in fact or in the aspirations of the great majority of Americans. Furthermore, with no socialist party of any significance in the United States, the working class lacks that belief in government ownership of the means of production that is so widely accepted [where] a strong socialist tradition [exists].

This absence of a visible socialist movement in the United States affects not only our understanding of the newer nations of the world who seem to be heading in the direction of some kind of state enterprise and control, but it also makes us wary of the older, already industrialized nations of the world, like England, France and Japan. . . .

If our history is a poor guide for understanding the world today, it is also an obstacle to the world's understanding of us. Self-righteous Northerners too often assume that the subordination of the Negro in American culture is an unfortunate, but largely Southern phenomenon, not typical of our society as a whole. To any objective observer, though, it is evident that throughout history, down to the present, the black man has been a problem for white Americans, north as well as south of Mason's and Dixon's line. For a long time in our history, because the Negro was a slave, the question of his proper place in society was ignored. But even as Northerners argued against slavery in the South in the years before the Civil War, it was evident that opposition to slavery did not mean that the black man was accepted as an equal with the white. . . .

Thus when the newly emergent peoples of the world, nearly all of whom are colored, criticize the American attitude toward the Negro, they are doing more than merely objecting to the treatment they might receive here. They are objecting to our history; they are finding in us a deficiency that is not in the nature of man but in the nature of our history. It might, after all, have been different. Therefore, despite all our good intentions and regardless of the correctness of the Supreme Court's decisions, our slowness in eradicating racial discrimination is as difficult for the colored peoples in the world to understand as their political and economic backwardness is for us.

There is yet another burden that the past places upon Americans in confronting the world of the mid-twentieth century. Leaders in a contest of global dimensions are expected to have a philosophy, an ideology, for by having one they can make their aims clear and they can attract followers. America, though, as Daniel Boorstin has pointed out, lacks an ideology. The new life and new ways of thought that Americans like to think they brought into being on this continent are the result not of plan or ideology, but of circumstances. As the example of the Revolution reminds us, Americans look to a political utopia in the past, not in the future. We talk of progress in material things, but rarely do we talk of political progress, although we frequently lament the sorry decline in the level of our political behavior. . . . The whole structure of our political life is pragmatic and without plan. Our political parties have always been collections of diverse interests and only by the greatest of effort have historians and political scientists been able to find differences between them. . . .

The fact is that we have no ideology, for by definition an ideology is capable of being made universal. Our peculiar history cannot be spelled out, attractively packaged and sold to people with a quite different historical experience. In this respect we are at a grave disadvantage in the world struggle of ideas with communism. Communism, after all, was designed as an ideology and only later was forcibly adapted to the circumstances and uses of a single country, or, more recently, several countries. Here, too, our history has been of no help.

It has often been observed that, from the time of the first Puritans down to the days of the New Frontier, Americans have been a people with a sense of mission. But the mission has been neither a proselytizing nor an aggressive one. . . . Despite the rhetoric of . . . propagandists for support of the Revolutionary War effort, the founding fathers were convinced of the essential differences between America and the rest of the world. . . .

Lincoln, echoing a remark of Jefferson's, called America the last, best hope of man. For most of the nineteenth century, the mission of America was what could be achieved here, not what could be exported to other peoples. If the downtrodden peasant of Central Europe or the unfranchised worker of a London slum wished to realize the dream for which America stood, he was not urged to reproduce America in his own country, but to come here. And does not this belief that America is unique, that the mission is to create the city on the hill, help to explain that tendency of Americans to reproduce their home environment wherever they may be . . . ?

There was a time, undoubtedly, when our awareness of the unique character of our history was tinged, if not suffused, with a sense of superiority. My purpose has not been to perpetuate that feeling; the object in emphasizing the unique features of the American past does not stem from any sense of arrogant pride. The aim has been quite different. In an age when America is a model for the whole world, it is important for us to remember that our history is irrelevant for most other peoples. If we do remember that then we will not expect other nations to follow our path and will save ourselves from disappointment arising out of misjudgment.

Frequently in our history the unique character of the American past was used as a support for isolation from the rest of the world. But that has not been my intention, either. No nation, least of all the United States, is an island unto itself in the present world. Nevertheless, the burdens that our peculiar history places upon us as an international leader should not be ignored, or, as some would try to do, speciously transmuted into assets. Our history has neither fitted us for nor warned us of the international role that now we play. In this restricted, if important sense, our history is a burden to us and irrelevant to the future of others.

The Genius of American Politics*

Daniel J. Boorstin

The author is Professor of American History at the University of Chicago and has been a visiting scholar at various universities in Italy, France,

---

*Reprinted from Daniel J. Boorstin, *The Genius of American Politics* (Chicago: University of Chicago Press, 1953), pp. 181–89, with the permission reserved. Copyright 1953 under the International Copyright Union. Published of the publisher. Copyright 1953 by The University of Chicago. All rights 1953. Composed and printed by The University of Chicago Press, Chicago 37, Illinois, U.S.A.

Puerto Rico, and Japan. Of American birth, after receiving his baccalaureate he became a Rhodes Scholar at Oxford, taking a coveted Double First. He has also been admitted to the bar in England (Barrister-at-law, Inner Temple, London) and in the United States.

The doom which awaited the Roman Empire, according to C. N. Cochrane, "was that of a civilization which failed to understand itself and was, in consequence, dominated by a haunting fear of the unknown." Much the same could be said for us. Our intellectual insecurity, our feeling of philosophical inadequacy, may be explained at least in part by our failure to understand ourselves. This failure is due in some measure to our readiness to accept the European clichés about us.

We all know that people are prone to parade their weaknesses as if they were virtues. Anyone who has recently been among Europeans can tell you that there is an increasing tendency on the old continent to blame the United States for lacking many of the ills which have characterized European history. Our lack of poverty is called materialism, our lack of political dogma is called aimlessness and confusion. On the whole, the people, and especially the intellectuals of Europe, who are desperately on the offensive, have succeeded in convincing us—and especially our intellectuals. They have made us apologize for our wealth and welfare. You will find many well-meaning Americans abroad who think that they are defending their country when they point out that people in the United States are really a lot worse off than Europeans think. They have made us apologize for our lack of philosophical clarity, so that we seek to concoct a political philosophy which can rival the dogmas of Europe.

It has been too long since we have stood on the special virtues of our life and our continent. Over a century has passed since Emerson declared in his "American Scholar": "Our day of dependence, our long apprenticeship to the learning of other lands, draws to a close. The millions that around us are rushing into life, cannot always be fed on the mere remains of foreign harvests." But we still see ourselves in the distorting mirror of Europe.

The image which Europe shows us is as much a defense of itself as a caricature of us. We are too easily persuaded that the cancers of European life (and especially of European political life) are healthy growths and that we are deformed for not possessing them.

The equations of poverty and idealism, of monopoly and responsibility, of aristocracy and culture, of political dogma and purposeful political institutions, are too readily accepted. It is, of course, some solace to a declining European culture—a culture dying of poverty, monopoly, aristocracy, and ideology—to think that their ills are simply the excess of their virtues. That theirs must be the virtues of all cultures. And hence that the accidents of history which may have immunized us against such vices also sterilize our culture and doom us to philistinism and vagrancy.

There is no denying that our intellectuals and, most of all, our academics, being the most cosmopolitan part of our culture, have been especially susceptible to the well-meaning advice of our sick friends in Europe. Like many sick friends, they are none too sorry to be able to tell us that we are not in the best of health.

We have, in a word, been too easily led to deny our peculiarly American virtues, in order to seem to have the peculiar European vices. Moreover, our intellectuals, who rightly consider themselves the critical organ of our community, have been much too sensitive to any charge of chauvinism. Hence they, too, have been readier to tell us what we lack than to help us discover what we have. Our historians and political scientists, while blaming themselves and one another for "irresponsibility," have failed to help us discover the peculiar virtues of our situation. They have left the discovery and defense of those virtues to the dubious efforts of professional patriots.

Is it any wonder that the very word "patriotism" should come to be suspect among intellectuals? Is it any wonder that we suffer from cultural hypochondria?

The cure for our hypochondria is surely not chauvinism. That simply adds one real ill to the many unreal ills of which we already accuse ourselves. Waving a flag cannot cure inner uncertainty. One possibility, at least a little more fruitful, is to try to discover the peculiar virtues of our situation, the special character of our history: to try to judge ourselves by the potentialities of our own peculiar and magnificent continent. We may then discover that our virtues, like our ills, are actually peculiar to ourselves; that what seem to be inadequacies of our culture, if measured by European standards, are nothing but our differences and may even be virtues. . . .

The European concept of culture is basically aristocratic; its great successes—especially in countries like Italy and France—are in the aristocratic arts. Its literature is for the few; its newspapers are subsidized by political parties; its books, when successful, have a circulation a fifth of that in America, even in proportion to the population. European culture, most of it at least, is the heritage of a pre-liberal past. For all their magnificence, the monuments of that past are products of a culture with which we, fortunately, are in no position to compete. It is surely no accident that we have accomplished relatively little in the arts of painting, sculpture, palace and church architecture, chamber music, and chamber poetry. It is equally no accident that we have contributed so little in political philosophy.

Some Americans, however—and they are probably increasing in number—make un-American demands for a philosophy of democracy. They believe that this philosophy will be a weapon against Russia and a prop for our own institutions. They are afraid that, without some such salable commodity, they may not be able to compete with Russia in the world market.

These people are puzzled that we should have come as far as we have without knowing the philosophy which lies beneath our institutions. They are even frightened at what they might find—or fail to find—when they open the *sanctum sanctorum* of national belief. It is these who are among our most dangerous friends; for, even if they should find the Holy of Holies empty, they would refuse to admit it. Instead of trying to discover the reasons why we have managed to be free of idolatry, they will make their own graven image, their own ass's head, and say that is what belonged in the temple all the time. These people are dangerous because they would misrepresent us abroad and corrupt us at home.

If we have no exportable political theory, then can we export our political institutions? Should we try to induce the Italian or the German people to become democratic in the American image? If the thesis of this book is correct, the answer here too is, of course, No. The answer is No, not merely because the attempt to distill our philosophy or to transplant our institutions is apt to fail. It is No, because the principles on which we approach politics and have succeeded in building our own institutions, deny such a possibility.

If we have learned anything from our history, it is the wisdom of allowing institutions to develop according to the needs of each particular environment; and the value of both environmentalism and traditionalism as principles of political life, as ways of saving ourselves from the imbecilities, the vagaries, and the cosmic enthusiasms of individual men. This is our idea of constitutional federalism, without which our great union would have been impossible.

If what has held us together as a nation has been no explicit political theory held in common but rather a fact of life (what Whitman properly called "adhesiveness"), how can we expect to bind other nations by theories? We have felt both "individualism which isolates" and, as he says, "adhesiveness or love, that fuses, ties, and aggregates."

We have traditionally held out to the world, not our doctrine, but our example. The idea of America as the last best hope of mankind has not been the idea that America would outdo other ages and places with its philosophy. It was life, and not thought, which would excel here. This has perhaps taken some of the sting of arrogance out of our consciousness of destiny. For men are in the habit of claiming more personal credit for the quality of their thought than for the quality of their institutions. Even to the most obtuse, institutions seem the product of many forces. In the past we have wanted to be judged not by what we could tell the world but by what we could show the world. Moreover, we have considered ourselves not a factory of institutions but a laboratory, an experiment. By showing what man might do under our new circumstances, we might give men everywhere new hope for improving their lot after their own fashion.

No one has stated the case better than did John C. Calhoun, speaking at the time of the Mexican War, about a century ago:

> It has been lately urged in a very respectable quarter, that it is the mission of this country to spread civil and religious liberty over all the globe, and especially over this continent—even by force, if necessary. It is a sad delusion. . . . It is a remarkable fact in the political history of man, that there is scarcely an instance of a free constitutional government, which has been the work exclusively of foresight and wisdom. They have all been the result of a fortunate combination of circumstances (*Works*, IV, 416).

It is our experience, not our dogma or our power, that may be the encouragement and the hope of the world. We can, Calhoun concluded, "do more to extend liberty by our example over the country and the world generally, than would be done by a thousand victories."

To tell people what institutions they must have, whether we tell them with the Voice of America or with the Money of America, is the thorough denial of our American heritage. It would be an attempt "to meet the monolithic East by attempting to set up a monolithic West." As Stephen Spender has observed, "When the Communists today congratulate themselves on being 'monolithic,' they are congratulating themselves in being dead: and it is for us to see that they do not turn the whole world into their cemetery." An imposed democracy expresses a corroding cynicism. And democratic institutions, however much they may rest on pessimism, must be the opposite of cynical. Tyrannies—fascism, naziism, communism—can impose themselves on others with no hypocrisy, for they rest unashamedly on force. But if we were to become cynical in order to make Europe seem to stand for something better than it might on its own, we would risk losing everything, even if we should win.

Is it not even possible that the people of Europe will be more willing to defend themselves if it is their own institutions they are defending? If they are unwilling to defend their own, they surely will not want to defend ours.

We have, of course, our modern abolitionists, those who believe that the abolition of slavery in Russia is the sole issue in the world. They surely need no philosophy. The clarity and righteousness of their objective is enough. Soviet communism provides them the sense of "giveness," of obviousness in their objective. For them, Communists embody the spirit of Satan as vividly as the American Indians did for the first Puritans, or as the southern slaveowners did for fire-eaters like Phillips and Garrison. Some of them would seem almost as willing as Garrison to burn the Constitution in order to attain their admirable objective.

There are others who take a more practical Lincolnian view. Like Lincoln, these people hate slavery anywhere, but they doubt their capacity to make a perfect world. Their main concern is to preserve and improve free institutions where they now exist.

If the Lincolnian view involves us in the seeming contradiction of defending our institutions without insisting on propagating them, this is nothing but the contradiction within the idea of freedom itself, which affirms a value but asserts it only to allow a competition among values. We must refuse to become crusaders for liberalism, in order to remain liberals. We must refuse to try to export our commodity. We must refuse to become crusaders for conservatism, in order to conserve the institutions and the genius which have made America great.

Democracy Isn't Always Exportable*

Lucius Beebe

Lucius Beebe was author, journalist, newspaper publisher, and authority on American railroad history. In his last years as a newspaper columnist of great style and wit, he wrote on a variety of subjects.

The persistent notion that great numbers of people in other parts of the world want to live by the same social and political standards as do citizens of the United States or, if they don't want to, ought to, is a national delusion that dies hard.

The source of our national grief, and one that grows in intensity as the melancholy record unfolds, is that despite our tireless plugging of the commodity for now nigh unto two centuries, there are very few buyers for the peculiar institution of political democracy. Here and there a few reluctant folk are conned into making a down payment on what they patently regard as a dubious bill of goods to begin with, but few of them come through after the down payment and almost none consummate the full purchase.

Americans have spent uncounted billions and great reserves of energy to promote democracy wherever they could get a hearing and in many places where the reception was explicitly hostile. Democracy for export has been entrusted to the highest priced salesmen available to our national resources, the ultimate hard sell having been undertaken as a strictly tie-in deal by Woodrow Wilson with his slogan about "making the world safe for democracy."

The tie-in price was America's participation on the Allied side in a losing war against the Central Powers. To get the Yanks over

---

*Reprinted by permission of the publisher. Copyright 1965, Chronicle Features, San Francisco.

there, all Europe had to do was to stand and uncover at mention of American egalitarian principles. Final delivery was, however, rejected with gestures, and Wilson himself soon provided the most conspicuous death of a salesman on record.

In historic fact American democracy is an import from France at the time of the French Revolution. It worked better in the United States than it did in France which almost immediately had second thoughts in the matter and reverted to a wild succession of imperial adventures alternating with quasi-popular administrations, and there are those who see a clear similarity between the current French government and the First Empire of Napoleon.

The whole imported idea flourished in the United States and, with obvious modifications, has worked well ever since. Its justification, of course, has not been any fundamental virtue in the basic philosophy of democratic conduct, but a fantastically opulent economy that would have financed any social experiment that contrived to become associated with it.

The success of democracy in the continental United States has given Americans in their relations with people of other nationalities a messianic fixation of moral superiority and, until very recently when it became apparent that the project is a bust, has evolved attempted tie-in sales of American political thinking along with nationally financed benevolences, such as dams, electric power projects, and military reorganizations. You could have a splendid new railway system if you adopted the secret ballot, or malaria control was available if you bought universal suffrage.

Largely, while the basic export assets were gladly accepted, the contingent bonus packages were returned without opening, in Asia, Latin America and Africa emphatically, and more courteously but with equal firmness, in Europe.

That democracy isn't a universal condition of life or even, in many places a thinkable one, is a distressing idea to Americans.

American partisans of democracy could, if they would, learn a lesson from the fate of American religious missionaries who made a dreadful nuisance of themselves in Asia and Africa in the Nineteenth Century when they undertook to spread the Christian gospel accompanied by the moral prejudices of Circleville, Ohio, to large numbers of contented people already far gone in the practical satisfactions of pagan sin. The plumper and younger missionaries end as the chef's blue plate suggestion, which served them right.

American exports of a more tangible nature in the last few decades have proven enormously more acceptable than the Christian ethic or a republican political philosophy. Heaven knows, most of them have been an affront to civilization; high rise hotels, cola drinks, television and radio sets and their accompanying mental climate, sports attire, le jazz hot, Marlon Brando, ball point styluses and can-of-worms traffic intersections. Most of them are abominations and their advent as explicit a manifestation of the advent of barbarism as the advance scout of Attila the Hun.

But, unlike our holier endeavors and more sanctimonious articles of faith for export, they don't arouse hostility and desecretion on a universal scale. It may yet be that Conrad Hilton is a better salesman for the American way than Woodrow Wilson. It's a sobering thought.

Chapter Three

The American Democracy as Myth and Mission for Americanization

The American adventure in the Pacific began with the Spanish-American War and has continued through two world wars. From the instances of the Philippine and Japanese occupations, almost fifty years apart, we may gain a special perspective on our impact abroad, for in both cases we undertook to institute American-style self government.

Senator Lodge defended our take-over of the Philippines by citing our occupation of the Louisiana Territory, another region of diverse peoples, without the consent of the governed. We did spread democracy by our rule, but we also extended our markets. Was the latter purely incidental to the former? The issues discussed in the previous section bear on this question.

Stanley Karnow, a recent visitor to the Philippines, sees our effect on those islands as a "bewildering collision" of native and borrowed features after half a century of intimate contact with the United States. In the case of Japan, Richard Hughes suggests that there may be considerable truth in the idea that this vigorous people has actually absorbed us; the Americanization of the Japanese is only part of the picture.

In the person of General Douglas MacArthur, we have a beloved hero who figured importantly in both the Philippines and Japan. His letter to the American people asserts that our performance in these countries has been completely consistent with our ideals. Our principles of government seemed readily applicable to Japan; MacArthur expected the Japanese to accept them willingly. Nevertheless, our dealings with these countries in a complicated import–export relationship remains an uneasy issue for many Americans.

The Philippine Islands (1900)

Henry Cabot Lodge

Henry Cabot Lodge (1850–1924) was first a Congressman (1886) and then a Senator (1893) from Massachusetts. Until his death in 1924, he was a powerful Republican leader in state and national affairs. He championed American expansion in the Caribbean and the Pacific, and successfully led the fight against President Wilson's campaign for American entry into the League of Nations after World War I. This speech was given before the Senate on March 7, 1900.

. . . I hope and believe that we shall retain the islands, and that, peace and order once restored, we shall and should reestablish civil government, beginning with the towns and villages, where the inhabitants are able to manage their own affairs. We should give them honest administration, and prompt and efficient courts. We should see to it that there is entire protection to persons and property, in order to encourage the development of the islands by the assurance of safety to investors of capital. All men should be protected in the free exercise of their religion, and the doors thrown open to missionaries of all Christian sects. The land, which belongs to the people, and of which they have been robbed in the past, should be returned to them and their titles made secure. We should inaugurate and carry forward, in the most earnest and liberal way, a comprehensive system of popular education. Finally, while we bring prosperity to the islands by developing their resources, we should, as rapidly as conditions will permit, bestow upon them self-government and home rule. . . .

Our opponents put forward as their chief objection that we have robbed these people of their liberty and have taken them and hold them in defiance of the doctrine of the Declaration of Independence in regard to the consent of the governed. As to liberty, they have never had it, and have none now, except when we give it to them protected by the flag and the armies of the United States. Their insurrection against Spain, confined to one island, has been utterly abortive and could never have revived or been successful while Spain controlled the sea. We have given them all the liberty they ever had. We could not have robbed them of it, for they had none to lose.

The second objection as to the consent of the governed requires more careful examination. We must go a step farther and see how the American people throughout their history have applied this principle to the vast territory which they have acquired. Under the guidance of Thomas Jefferson, and with a Congress obedient to his slightest behest, we took Louisiana without the consent of the governed, and ruled it without their consent so long as we saw fit.

A few years more passed, and, in 1819, we bought Florida from Spain without the consent of the governed. Then came the Mexican war, and by the treaty of Guadalupe Hidalgo we received a great cession of territory from Mexico, including all the California coast; and although we paid Mexico twenty millions as indemnity I think it has been held that the cession was one of conquest. There were many Mexicans living within the ceded territory. We never asked their consent. In 1867 we purchased Alaska from Russia, territory, people and all. It will be observed that to the white inhabitants we allow the liberty of returning to Russia, but we except the uncivilized tribes specifically. They are to be governed without their consent, and they are not even to be allowed to become citizens.

If the arguments which have been offered against our taking the Philippine Islands because we have not the consent of the inhabitants be just, then our whole past record of expansion is a crime. I do not think that we violated in that record the principles of the Declaration of Independence. On the contrary, I think we spread them over regions where they were unknown. . . .

The next argument of the opponents of the Republican policy is that we are denying self-government to the Filipinos. Our reply is that to give independent self-government at once, as we understand it, to a people who have no just conception of it and no fitness for it, is to dower them with a curse instead of a blessing. To do this would be to entirely arrest their progress instead of advancing them on the road to the liberty and free government which we wish them to achieve and enjoy. This contention rests, of course, on the proposition that the Filipinos are not today in the least fitted for self-government, as we understand it.

We have been told that arguments like these are sordid. Sordid indeed! Then what arguments are worthy of consideration? A policy which proposes to open wider markets to the people of the United States, to add to their employment, and to increase their wages, and which in its pursuit requires that we should save the teeming millions of China from the darkness of the Russian winter, and keep them free, not merely for the incoming of commerce, but for the entrance of the light of Western civilization, seems to me a great and noble policy, if there ever was such, and one which may well engage the best aspirations and the highest abilities of American statesmanship.

Thus, Mr. President, I have shown that duty and interest alike, duty of the highest kind and interest of the highest and best kind, impose upon us the retention of the Philippines, the development of the islands, and the expansion of our Eastern commerce. All these things, in my belief, will come to pass, whatever the divisions of the present moment, for no people who have come under our flag have ever sought to leave it, and there is no territory which we have acquired that any one would dream of giving up.

All our vast growth and expansion have been due to the spirit of our race, and have been guided by the instinct of the American people, which in all great crises has proved wiser than any reasoning. This mighty movement westward, building up a nation and conquering a continent as it swept along, has not been the work of chance or accident. It was neither chance nor accident which brought us to the Pacific and which has now carried us across the great ocean even to the shores of Asia, to the very edge of the cradle of the Aryans, whence our far distant ancestors started on the march which has since girdled the world.

Like every great nation, we have come more than once in our history to where the road of fate divided. Thus far we have never failed to take the right path. Again are we come to the parting of the ways. Again a momentous choice is offered to us. Shall we hesitate and make, in coward fashion, what Dante calls "the great refusal"?

Even now we can abandon the Monroe Doctrine, we can reject the Pacific, we can shut ourselves up between our oceans, as Switzerland is inclosed among her hills, and then it would be inevitable that we should sink out from among the great powers of the world and heap up riches that some stronger and bolder people, who do not fear their fate, might gather them. Or we may follow the true laws of our being, the laws in obedience to which we have come to be what we are, and then we shall stretch out into the Pacific; we shall stand in the front rank of the world powers; we shall give to our labor and our industry new and larger and better opportunities; we shall prosper ourselves; we shall benefit mankind. What we have done was inevitable because it was in accordance with the laws of our being as a nation, in the defiance and disregard of which lie ruin and retreat.

The Bewildering Collision*

Stanley Karnow

Mr. Karnow is an experienced commentator on Asian affairs. He lives in Hong Kong and is a *Washington Post* correspondent.

An American visiting the Philippines is apt to experience a strange shock of recognition. For a half-century of United States colonial tutelage, generously administered and gracefully relinquished in 1946, seems to have fashioned the Philippines into a mirror of America. But the reflection it casts can be deceptive. Nothing is more disappointing to Americans than the discovery, often belated, that "our little brown brothers," as imperial propaganda used to call them, are only superficial relatives.

Americans are often led astray by the outward signs of resemblance. Manila looks in many ways, like a sprawling, unwieldy city in the United States. Its traffic-clogged avenues are blighted by billboards proclaiming American merchandise in high-pitched Madison Avenue jargon; sleazy drive-ins offer "colossal" hot dogs, hamburgers, and other gastronomic imitations. Manila's suburbs, with their split-level ranch houses, and California haciendas, rival Beverly Hills; its slums outdo Harlem. And many educated, urbane Filipinos appear more Americanized than any American.

---

*Reprinted from *The Saturday Review* (October 8, 1966), with the permission of author and publisher.

Gentlemen with names like cigar brands—Benedicto, Modesto, Eugenio—are known to their pals as "Butch" and "Baby," and they have an extraordinary capacity for behaving like Babbitts. They are avid golfers, earnest Rotarians, and proud students of "human relations" as taught by a local branch of the Dale Carnegie Institute. Nothing is quite so disarming as to wander into a luncheon of the Junior Chamber of Commerce in a provincial town: the speeches might have been written in Cedar Rapids, even if the delivery is rather reminiscent of Wallace Beery playing Pancho Villa. Filipinos may speak dialects like Tagalog at home, but their public language is a kind of calypso American that would have delighted Mencken. Recently, reporting the mayor's investigation into police department complaints, a Manila newspaper headlined: "City Dad Probes Cops Gripes."

It is midsummer madness to hold Philippine weddings in June, when the heat and humidity are at their worst. Yet fashionable Filipinos must be "June brides," and they perspire heroically through all the functions which, incidentally, feature delicacies imported from the United States. Though there are 7,000 Philippine islands, Filipinos thrive on canned American salmon and tuna fish. Manila high society rejects local avocados and bananas as lower-class "native" fare. When the late General MacArthur, an authentic Philippine folk-hero, visited Manila a few years ago, a banquet at the presidential palace opened with tinned American fruit salad.

Thus this Philippine mirror of America is a kind of carnival mirror, casting distorted images. In contrast to Hawaii, where the process of American acculturation almost entirely assimilated a multiracial population, the Philippines was never transformed into a parcel of the United States by colonial rule. American influence in its Pacific territory set in motion the dynamics of political and economic change, while scarcely altering the country's deep social traditions. The Filipino may behave and speak like an American; he usually doesn't think like an American. The Filipinos recognize that they are currently caught in a bewildering collision between modern hopes and ancient habits. They are groping to establish an identity, and that search is likely to continue for some time to come.

Ethnically Malay, with doses of Chinese thrown in, the Filipinos were controlled by Spain for 350 years and by the United States until after World War II—or as they themselves quip: "Three centuries in a convent and two generations in Hollywood."

Spanish domination unified the thousands of Philippine islands and Christianized the people in much the same manner that the *conquistadores* brought Catholicism to Latin America. In its inexperienced, pragmatic way, American rule gave the country a different dimension. Even before the Philippine *insurrectos* were subdued about the turn of the century—at a cost of 4,000 American and an estimated 10,000 Philippine lives—the United States was considering eventual autonomy for its new possession. In a statement remarkably advanced for that period of history, an American commission recommended the establishment of local government "designed not for our satisfaction . . . but for the happiness, peace and prosperity of the people of the Philippine Islands, and the measures adopted should be made to conform to their customs, their habits, and even their prejudices. . . ."

As early as 1899, the Philippine Supreme Court was headed by a Filipino; by 1907, the Filipinos had their own legislature, though its proposals were subject to American veto. The number of Americans in the Philippine administration quickly diminished, from 51 per cent in 1903 to 6 per cent in 1923. Self-rule was largely made possible because of education, which the United States actively fostered. Soon after American rule began, more than 1,000 American schoolteachers arrived to fan out through the islands. Within twenty-five years, there were more high-school students in the Philippines than in Spain, the former mother country. If not for the advent of World War II, the Philippines would probably have gained total independence in the mid-1930's.

In retrospect, however, it may be debatable whether the rapid introduction of democracy into the Philippines was salutary, for a Western political system was accorded a people who, from their combined Oriental and Latin traditions, customarily consider public service a means to gain personal profit. As the Jesuit sociologist, Father Jaime Bulato, has explained, the Filipino's conduct is guided more by a sense of shame than of guilt; he would rather be judged guilty of corruption than feel ashamed for failing to dip into the government coffers to help his family. During the last election campaign, the charge by his political opponents, that President

Ferdinand Marcos had, as a youth, killed one of his father's rivals made little headway with Philippine voters. Even if he had been guilty, they reasoned,. Marcos had laudably acted to defend his father's honor.

American-inspired democracy in the Philippines, consequently, often suggests an exaggerated travesty of democracy that at times seems close to anarchy. Graft and corruption, nepotism, oratorical hyperbole—all these are parts of the Philippine political scene, very much as they characterized politics in the United States sixty or seventy years ago. There are even muck-raking Philippine journalists who reach back to Lincoln Steffens and Ray Stannard Baker for inspiration.

Another facet of United States rule is also having a current effect on the Philippines. As a few Filipinos now see it, the easy path to independence may have produced an oddly enervating result. In other colonial regions during the 1930's, budding nationalists were arming and agitating for self-government. The need for conflict was alien to Filipinos, however; they knew they were headed for freedom. But because they were pampered, many Filipinos now feel they failed to forge a solid sense of nationalism tempered by hardship and battle. They suspect that the vague "special relationship" that ties them to the United States is really a sequel to colonialism. One of the most thoughtful, articulate young Philippine politicians, Senator Raul Manglapus has said: "Our cart went before the horse. Others struggle for freedom before independence; we are struggling afterward. If we had had a brutal break with the United States, perhaps our relations today would be better."

In the days of United States colonial rule, Americans had a privileged market in the Philippines. Accordingly, American-manufactured goods flooded the islands, thwarting local incentives to industrialize. At the same time, the United States stimulated production of sugar, copra, hemp, and other export products until, by 1940, they represented about one-third of total Philippine income. The Philippines, therefore, typified the narrow "colonial" economy, reliant on the United States for survival. To a significant extent it still does: nearly half its export earnings depend upon special commercial accords with the U.S.

The American encouragement of export crops inadvertently caused more damaging consequences visible today. Favored by the

United States, traditional landlords expanded their estates to grow sugar and copra by grabbing marginal lands or dispossessing bankrupt farmers.

This rural degeneration has curiously evolved side-by-side with American development. Under the United States, natural resources were tapped and social services were expanded. Since 1946, Philippine war veterans have received more than a billon dollars in pensions and social security benefits. The American Air Force and Naval bases in the Philippines are a dual boon: they funnel dollars into the country, and they protect the Philippines, permitting the government to spend only 12 per cent of its budget on defense—and 35 per cent on education.

At this stage, however, many Filipinos apparently lack the patience or inclination to weigh the pros and cons of past colonialism. They are noisily, almost desperately, seeking to assert a national personality they have not yet formulated. They have tried, for instance, to shape a national language out of Tagalog, one of the country's eight major tongues. They have revived old heroes like General Emilio Aguinaldo, who led the *insurrectos*. They changed their national holiday from July 4 to June 12, the anniversary of an abortive republic founded in 1898. They have demonstrated against the American bases, and criticized commercial agreements that, in many respects, favor them. Local newspaper columnists have insulted the American ambassador, William McCormick Blair, Jr., and in a recent fit of pique, one of them derided Americans as "the most bigoted, narrow-minded sadistic race in the world."

A prominent Philippine leader, trying to assess much of his nationalist excitement, has described it as an effort by Filipinos to "shake themselves loose from Uncle Sam's shirttails." More cogently perhaps, a Manila editor has advanced the view that Filipinos are basically frustrated in their dream of becoming American. As he put it, they have been "Americanized" by books, radio, TV, and the movies, only to realize in the end that they are not Americans. "Their anti-American resentment is merely the other face of attraction," he wrote. "Filipinos would be Americans and cannot be."

But whatever Filipinos turn out to be will come from a long historical process that cannot be hastened by slogans and oratory. And whatever the final blend, it is bound to include a dash of American.

A Fourth of July Message (1947)*

General Douglas MacArthur

One of the most illustrious generals in American history, son of an equally famed general, Douglas MacArthur graduated from West Point Academy, where he later held the office of Superintendent, served as Commander of the Rainbow Division in World War I, Field Marshal of the Philippine Army, Supreme Commander of the Allied Powers in the Pacific, and Commander of United Nations forces in the Korean War. He served as an officer in the occupation forces in the Philippines after the Spanish–American War, in Germany after World War I, and was Supreme Commander of the Japanese occupation after World War II, where he oversaw the writing of the Japanese Constitution. A brilliant writer, speaker, and great patriot, he was a possible Republican presidential nominee several times during the period from World War II to his death in 1964. The speech was solicited and printed by *Life* magazine.

HEADQUARTERS OF SUPREME
COMMANDER OF ALLIED POWERS
TOKYO, JAPAN

Life has invited me, as an American standing on distant shores, to discuss the underlying significance of the Fourth of July and the events which it commemorates. I have been somewhat reluctant to do so as those ideals which form the pattern of our way of life are firmly rooted in the hearts of the American people from early age. Actuated by the thought, however, that perchance we who temporarily stand among an alien race of spiritual growth stunted by long tenure under the physical, mental and cultural strictures of feudalistic precepts—the very antitheses of American ideals—may see in contemporary events a more comprehensive significance than was either envisaged by their architects or is even now fully comprehended by Americans at home, I am enboldened to comment upon the international significance of the impact of the American

Life (July 4, 1947). Reprinted with the permission of the publisher.

concept of human relationship upon the fabric of civilized society as we here view it from distant shores.

Throughout the span of our national history we have thought of those rights and privileges and immunities, protections and equal opportunities, which have since our country's birth been safeguarded for use, as things peculiarly American. Content to live by the sacred tenets of freedom passed on from generation to generation, and to defend them in the forum of public debate or by the sword in the field if necessary, we have given little thought to the reality that our growth as a people, the development and progress of our free institutions, and the spiritual, physical and material strength which we as free men have mustered to repel every threat of destruction has had a profound and lasting influence not only upon our own lives but upon the entire human race as well.

Our experience in the Philippines and in the more recent reformation of Japanese life, where in reshaping the lives of others we have been guided by the same pattern from which is taken the design of our own lives, offers unmistakable proof that while American in origin and American in concept, these tenets underlying a truly free society are no less designed to secure, preserve and advance the well-being of one race than another—and given the opportunity to take root in one society they will flourish and grow as surely as they will in any other society. The lesson from past and contemporary events is that they are no longer peculiarly American but now belong to the entire human race—and that their firm adaptability to the pattern of human life is by no means governed by ethnological considerations. The term "democracy" is now being subjected to conflicting connotations but American democracy for nearly two centuries has emerged triumphant from the successive crises of war and peace—and in every test it has established its soundness in comparison with every other philosophy which has governed the lives of men. A spiritual force whose purity of purpose is doubted by none, it has demonstrated in the American experience of blending men of all races and cultures into a composite whole that it can thrive in any heart and raise all who embrace it to a higher dignity and more useful purpose.

In the inception of Japan's reformation many voices were raised against the planned implantation here of ideals and principles and standards underlying American democracy. It was contended that

Japanese tradition, Japanese culture, and Japanese experience would not permit their assimilation in Japan's redesigned social system. Never was a statement more erroneous and unrealistic. For those very things which have supported Japan's past are responsible for the tragedy of Japan's present, and those very things which have supported America's past are no less responsible for the strength of America's present. This is well within the knowledge of the average Japanese citizen who is reaching out to understand and embrace those same concepts which have brought individual and collective strength, dignity and security to the American people —and once the process of assimilation has been completed, the Japanese may be expected to adhere to, cherish and preserve this new way of life.

The world has just emerged from the convulsive violence of war in which all humanity has been engaged or felt some impact. Now it struggles to adjust itself to the realization of peace. War's genesis lies in the despotic lust for power—frequently its rallying media for intense nationalism renders it the last refuge of the despot whose power is threatened from within. Never has it originated in the voluntary action of a free people; never will a free people voluntarily associate itself with the proposition that the road to peace and well-being and happiness lies through the crucible of war.

In the struggle for peace in which we are now engaged, the world finds itself half enslaved and half free as the clash of conflicting ideologies continues to stir mankind. True, the guns remain silent, but silent they will not long remain if avarice and greed and lust for power continue to dominate human relations, and the efforts of peoples who desire to live in peace and harmony with others and to erect a higher plane of civilization for the future are thwarted at the councils of the nations of the world by individuals or minorities, out of step with human progress, who would risk civilization's destruction rather than yield in their lust for further and more absolute power—intolerant of the rights of others in denying the very essence of human justice. Peace will be retarded and the imminence of war advanced, so long as depotism governs men's lives and reaches out to bring the lives of other peoples within its orbit of human enslavement—so long as the individual or the few, by the threat or application of force, may control the lives and destinies of the many—so long as knowledge is perverted and personal liberty suppressed.

It is for us in this era of confusion and uncertainty following the cataclysm of history's most violent struggle, calmly to refortify our lives and free institutions by rededication of ourselves to those ideals and principles and human standards which have guided our progress as a people; and while always mindful of our own business, fearlessly to discharge our responsibility to others, that by example we may point the way to a peaceful world of workable human relationships. Therein lies the best hope for overwhelming those evil forces which now plague mankind and for real advancement in human progress.

The Orientalization of the West*

Richard Hughes

Mr. Hughes, a native of Australia, lives in Hong Kong. He is a correspondent for the *London Sunday Times* and *The Economist.*

I can't go along with all this talk about the "Americanization" of the Far East. Indeed, the longer I live and move around in the Far East the more apprehensive I become of the ultimate "Orientalization" of the West.

All the alleged evidence of U.S. influence on the Far Eastern scene and the Asian way of life seems to me to be brittle, shallow, and misleading or misinformed. I am not echoing the old Matthew Arnold line about "the Far East bowing low before the blast in patient distain, letting the legions thunder past and plunging into thought again." These days, the East doesn't "plunge into thought again": it either plunges into violence, tries to continue dozing quietly in a corner, or struggles toward a higher living standard.

The world's technological revolution, for the time being, is transforming Asia—urban Asia—largely by proxy and by indirection. Certainly modernization is coming from the West—although Japan is increasingly getting into the act—but the great changes basically owe nothing to, and reflect nothing of, nationality, racialism, or

*Reprinted from *The Saturday Review* (October 8, 1966), with the permission of author and publisher.

ideology. An Asian doesn't have to sing "The Star-Spangled Banner" because he eats a hamburger or chews gum. American contributions to modernized life, from Coca-Cola to computing machines and from supermarkets to washing machines, appeal because of their merit and quality, not because of their origin—sometimes, in fact, in spite of their origin. Their acceptance, and imitation, does not impose American philosophic, political, social, or cultural values, good or bad, on local communities; but it reflects local aspirations for a happier life, limited by the local degree of affluence, local good fortune in foreign aid, and local immunity to or protection from evangelical Communism.

When I first went to Japan, before Pearl Harbor, I met English expatriates who deplored the fact that young Japanese had become interested in baseball rather than cricket. They felt that cricket would have made the Japanese pro-British, while baseball would make them pro-American—which was almost as bad as being pro-Japanese. In the same way, I daresay, German expatriates regretted that they had not taken up dueling, which might have made them more pro-German.

Tojo's abominable *kempei-tai* (military gendarmes) went along with this nonsense by trying vainly to stop young Japanese baseballers from using American terms such as *play* (or *pray*) *bollu* and *striku-one*. It was forgotten that when Japan decided to "modernize" under Emperor Meiji, its leaders modeled the navy on the Royal Navy, the army on the Prussian model, law on the Napoleonic Code, and business on the American pattern, and produced a completely and aggressively Japanese amalgam of all these foreign influences. The best *kamikaze* pilots were distinguished for their physical condition, which meant that most of them played baseball, without becoming noticeably Americanized.

With growing and hard-won affluence, the Japanese have since led the way with Asian adoption and adaptation of U. S. techniques, products, expertise, and ideas. They are now, in fact, retaliating successfully, exporting Japanese architecture and design to the United States, and motorcars, motorcycles, oil tankers, and transistor radios to all world markets. They even seem to be doing better, in reprisal, with Zen Buddhism abroad than the Christians are doing with Christianity inside Japan.

The modern face-lift in Japan is plain to see, and very Americanized it looks. But it represents no change of heart. A smart young

Japanese will drink whisky instead of *sake.* A *botto doggu* is often preferred to *sushi.* The girls' legs are straighter and their bosoms rounder, and geisha are playing golf. The three ancient Imperial Treasures were the Stone, the Mirror, and the Jewel; they have been replaced by the Car, the Refrigrator, and the TV set. (The Australians are now intervening with subversive "Australianization": P.R. experts are teaching the sons of *samurai* to eat meat-pies.) But, obscured or disguised, most of the basic traditions persist in Japan: The family groups, the neighborhood associations and honorable employment organizations still dominate life and living. Two of three young Japanese men still prefer to marry by arrangement—*miai*—either through their parents or one of the new "marriage advice counsel bureaus." Fewer Japanese girls are marrying *gaijin* (foreigners).

I recall one glittering U.S. reception in the heady days of General MacArthur's benevolent Occupation. The velvety lawns were jammed with respectful masses of what the Supreme Commander was wont to describe felicitously in official declarations as "the indigenous personnel." "I knew we would win the peace as well as the war," a high-ranking U.S. commander remarked to me. "The Japs have learned to appreciate our way of life. They recognize democracy. They're not fools—I've always said that. They learn. We'll build an American-style freedom and civilization here." His honest face was beaming with unselfish delight as he gulped bourbon.

Behind us, two charming middle-aged Japanese ladies in *kimono* halted to accept with deep bows some more U.S. army-issue orange juice. They were chatting casually in Japanese with the same rash abandon of Westerners in the Far East who assume that no Asians within earshot can understand English. "I do believe," one observed, "that the type of Occupation officer we are getting now has a less brutal and criminal type of face than those who came here in 1945." Her companion, inclining her head gracefully to my officer companion, suggested: "Or perhaps it is that we are becoming more accustomed to the faces?"

My friend saluted as they passed on. "Always show them respect," he adjured me. "It makes *them* respect *us.*"

The French failed in the same way to "Frenchify" Indochina. They left behind them a gracious legacy of elegant buildings, tree-lined boulevards, French bread and wine. But they left no Gallic imprint on the minds of the Vietnamese....

Chapter Four

The American Democracy as a Principle for Aid Doctrines

Aid to our allies and friends in the form of money, arms, and food is not a particularly new idea in the American experience. At various times since our revolutionary founding, we have sometimes covertly and sometimes openly assisted leaders and nations who emulated or aspired to our political (or economic) example. While old-style national rivalries in the post World War II world have by no means subsided, a new form of ideological competition, between so-called free and totalitarian governments for peoples' minds and political faiths has been fiercely pursued by means of aid programs. Increasingly in the postwar period, our presidents have spoken of exporting political ideals, institutions, and know-how as a desirable part of our modern strategy of aid. In 1947, President Truman extended American aid to Greece and her neighbors who were locked in an early Cold War struggle against the Soviet ideological and military threats then coming by way of Yugoslavia and Bulgaria. Truman even threatened to use military power to preserve the existing governments as President Monroe had done over a century before in Latin America, and as President Johnson has done in the middle 1960's in Southeast Asia. Public opinion, however, has often attacked this historic tactic. The late Senator Robert Taft argued that steps toward global aid would far more likely threaten liberty at home than advance welfare abroad.

Economic development requires certain institutions, incentives, and skills; even with the help of aid programs the economies of many of the new nations still seem to resist development. Reasonably stable governments are necessary for the growth of nations, but aid programs frequently induce socio-political changes, which may in turn precipitate revolutions to the detriment of individual liberty and happiness.

Must considerations of military security and economic policy have a necessary priority over those historically-professed American aims: liberty and self-determination for all peoples? On the other hand, must policies that flirt with traditional American isolationism, including withdrawal from South Vietnam, conflict with the American mission of liberty for all?

Pledges made by the President or his official spokesmen to foreign leaders have been considered by many to be binding national commitments. On April 19, 1966, Vice-President Humphrey said that in the Honolulu Conference, the United States made "a pledge to ourselves and to posterity to defeat aggression, to defeat social misery, to build viable, free political institutions and achieve peace" in Vietnam. Some Senators and a sizable number of citizens are troubled by the developing political struggle between the President and the Senate over key constitutional issues in the conduct of foreign policy.

The Truman Doctrine (1947)*

Harry S. Truman

Harry S. Truman achieved national prominence, while Senator from Missouri, as chairman of the Senate Committee to Investigate the National Defense Program, and he was Franklin Roosevelt's choice as Vice-President in 1944. Upon Roosevelt's death, Truman succeeded to the Presidency April 12, 1945. Against what appeared to be overwhelming Republican sentiment in the nation, he won election in 1948 with his Democratic Fair Deal program. His second term was concerned largely with the Cold War, the Marshall and Truman Plans, the Korean War, the organization of NATO, and the negotiation of the Japanese and German peace treaties. The Marshall Plan (1947), named after General George C. Marshall, Secretary of State in the Truman administration, aimed at the economic revival of Western Europe after the devastation of World War II "to permit the emergence of political and social conditions in which free institutions can exist." The Truman Plan (1949) outlined and began economic assistance to underdeveloped and communist-threatened nations throughout the world.

Mr. President, Mr. Speaker, Members of the Congress of the United States:

The gravity of the situation which confronts the world today necessitates my appearance before a joint session of the Congress.

---

*From the *Congressional Record,* March 12, 1947.

The foreign policy and the national security of this country are involved.

One aspect of the present situation, which I wish to present to you at this time for your consideration and decision, concerns Greece and Turkey.

The United States has received from the Greek government an urgent appeal for financial and economic assistance. Preliminary reports from the American economic mission now in Greece and reports from the American Ambassador in Greece corroborate the statement of the Greek government that assistance is imperative if Greece is to survive as a free nation.

I do not believe that the American people and the Congress wish to turn a deaf ear to the appeal of the Greek government.

Greece is not a rich country. Lack of sufficient natural resources has always forced the Greek people to work hard to make both ends meet. Since 1940, this industrious and peaceloving country has suffered invasion, four years of cruel enemy occupation, and bitter internal strife.

When forces of liberation entered Greece they found that the retreating Germans had destroyed virtually all the railways, roads, port facilities, communications, and merchant marine. More than a thousand villages had been burned. Eighty-five per cent of the children were tubercular. Livestock, poultry, and draft animals had almost disappeared. Inflation had wiped out practically all savings.

As a result of these tragic conditions, a militant minority, exploiting human want and misery, was able to create political chaos which, until now, has made economic recovery impossible.

Greece is today without funds to finance the importation of those goods which are essential to bare subsistence. Under these circumstances the people of Greece cannot make progress in solving their problems of reconstruction. Greece is in desperate need of financial and economic assistance to enable it to resume purchases of food, clothing, fuel, and seeds. These are indispensable for the subsistence of its people and are obtainable only from abroad. Greece must have help to import the goods necessary to restore internal order and security so essential for economic and political recovery.

The Greek government has also asked for the assistance of experienced American administrators, economists, and technicians to insure that the financial and other aid given to Greece shall be used effectively in creating a stable and self-sustaining economy and in improving its public administration.

The very existence of the Greek state is today threatened by the terrorist activities of several thousand armed men, led by Communists, who defy the Government's authority at a number of points, particularly along the northern boundaries. A commission appointed by the United Nations Security Council is at present investigating disturbed conditions in northern Greece and alleged border violations along the frontier between Greece on the one hand and Albania, Bulgaria, and Yugoslavia on the other.

Meanwhile, the Greek government is unable to cope with the situation. The Greek army is small and poorly equipped. It needs supplies and equipment if it is to restore the authority of the Government throughout Greek territory.

Greece must have assistance if it is to become a self-supporting and self-respecting democracy.

The United States must supply this assistance. We have already extended to Greece certain types of relief and economic aid but these are inadequate.

There is no other country to which democratic Greece can turn.

No other nation is willing and able to provide the necessary support for a democratic Greek government.

The British government, which has been helping Greece, can give no further financial or economic aid after March 31. Great Britain finds itself under the necessity of reducing or liquidating its commitments in several parts of the world, including Greece.

We have considered how the United Nations might assist in this crisis. But the situation is an urgent one requiring immediate action, and the United Nations and its related organizations are not in a position to extend help of the kind that is required.

It is important to note that the Greek government has asked for our aid in utilizing effectively the financial and other assistance we may give to Greece, and in improving its public administration. It is of the utmost importance that we supervise the use of any funds made available to Greece, in such a manner that each dollar spent will count toward making Greece self-supporting, and will help to build an economy in which a healthy democracy can flourish.

No government is perfect. One of the chief virtues of a democracy, however, is that its defects are always visible and under democratic processes can be pointed out and corrected. The government of Greece is not perfect. Nevertheless it represents 85 per cent of the members of the Greek parliament who were chosen in an election last year. Foreign observers, including 692 Americans, considered this election to be a fair expression of the views of the Greek people.

The Greek government has been operating in an atmosphere of chaos and extremism. It has made mistakes. The extension of aid by this country does not mean that the United States condones everything that the Greek government has done or will do. We have condemned in the past, and we condemn now, extremist measures of the right or the left. We have in the past advised tolerance, and we advise tolerance now.

Greece's neighbor, Turkey, also deserves our attention.

The future of Turkey as an independent and economically sound state is clearly no less important to the freedom-loving peoples of the world than the future of Greece. The circumstances in which Turkey finds itself today are considerably different from those of Greece. Turkey has been spared the disasters that have beset Greece. And during the war, the United States and Great Britain furnished Turkey with material aid.

Nevertheless, Turkey now needs our support.

Since the war Turkey has sought financial assistance from Great Britain and the United States for the purpose of effecting that modernization necessary for the maintenance of its national integrity.

That integrity is essential to the preservation of order in the Middle East.

The British government has informed us that, owing to its own difficulties, it can no longer extend financial or economic aid to Turkey.

As in the case of Greece, if Turkey is to have the assistance it needs, the United States must supply it. We are the only country able to provide that help.

I am fully aware of the broad implications involved if the United States extends assistance to Greece and Turkey, and I shall discuss these implications with you at this time.

One of the primary objectives of the foreign policy of the United States is the creation of conditions in which we and other nations will be able to work out a way of life free from coercion. This was a fundamental issue of the war with Germany and Japan. Our victory was won over countries which sought to impose their will, and their way of life, upon other nations.

To insure the peaceful development of nations, free from coercion, the United States has taken a leading part in establishing the United Nations. The United Nations is designed to make possible lasting freedom and independence for all its members. We shall not realize our objectives, however, unless we are willing to help free peoples to maintain their free institutions and their national integrity against aggressive movements that seek to impose upon them totalitarian regimes. This is no more than a frank recognition that totalitarian regimes imposed on free peoples, by direct or indirect aggression, undermine the foundations of international peace and hence the security of the United States.

The peoples of a number of countries of the world have recently had totalitarian regimes forced upon them against their will. The government of the United States has made frequent protests against coercion and intimidation, in violation of the Yalta agreement, in Poland, Rumania, and Bulgaria. I must also state that in a number of other countries there have been similar developments.

At the present moment in world history nearly every nation must choose between alternative ways of life. The choice is too often not a free one.

One way of life is based upon the will of the majority, and is distinguished by free institutions, representative government, free elections, guarantees of individual liberty, freedom of speech and religion, and freedom from political oppression.

The second way of life is based upon the will of a minority forcibly imposed upon the majority. It relies upon terror and oppression, a controlled press and radio, fixed elections, and the suppression of personal freedoms.

I believe that it must be the policy of the United States to support free peoples who are resisting attempted subjugation by armed minorities or by outside pressures.

I believe that we must assist free people to work out their own destinies in their own way.

I believe that our help should be primarily through economic and financial aid which is essential to economic stability and orderly political processes.

The world is not static and the status quo is not sacred. But we cannot allow changes in the status quo in violation of the Charter of the United Nations by such methods as coercion, or by such subterfuges as political infiltration.

In helping free and independent nations to maintain their freedom the United States will be giving effect to the principles of the Charter of the United Nations.

It is necessary only to glance at a map to realize that the survival and integrity of the Greek nation are of grave importance in a much wider situation. If Greece should fall under the control of an armed minority, the effect upon its neighbor, Turkey, would be immediate and serious. Confusion and disorder might well spread throughout the entire Middle East.

Moreover, the disappearance of Greece as an independent state would have a profound effect upon those countries in Europe whose peoples are struggling against great difficulties to maintain their freedoms and their independence while they repair the damages of war.

It would be an unspeakable tragedy if these countries, which have struggled so long against overwhelming odds, should lose that victory for which they sacrificed so much. Collapse of free institutions and loss of independence would be disastrous not only for them but for the world. Discouragement and possibly failure would quickly be the lot of neighboring peoples striving to maintain their freedom and independence.

Should we fail to aid Greece and Turkey in this fateful hour, the effect will be far reaching to the West as well as to the East.

We must take immediate and resolute action.

I therefore ask the Congress to provide authority for assistance to Greece and Turkey in the amount of $400 million for the period ending June 30, 1948. In requesting these funds, I have taken into consideration the maximum amount of relief assistance which would be furnished to Greece out of the $350 million which I recently requested that the Congress authorize for the prevention of starvation and suffering in countries devastated by the war.

In addition to funds, I ask Congress to authorize the detail of American civilian and military personnel to Greece and Turkey, at the request of those countries, to assist in the task of reconstruction, and for the purpose of supervising the use of such financial and material assistance as may be furnished. I recommend that authority also be provided for the instruction and training of selected Greek and Turkish personnel.

Finally, I ask that the Congress provide authority which will permit the speediest and most effective use, in terms of needed commodities, supplies, and equipment, of such funds as may be authorized.

If further funds, or further authority, should be needed for purposes indicated in this message, I shall not hesitate to bring the situation before the Congress. On this subject the executive and legislative branches of the government must work together.

This is a serious course upon which we embark.

I would not recommend it except that the alternative is much more serious.

The United States contributed $341 billion toward winning World War II. This is an investment in world freedom and world peace.

The assistance that I am recommending for Greece and Turkey amount to little more than one-tenth of 1 per cent of this investment. It is only common sense that we should safeguard this investment and make sure that it was not in vain.

The seeds of totalitarian regimes are nurtured by misery and want. They spread and grow in the evil soil of poverty and strife. They reach their full growth when the hope of a people for a better life has died.

We must keep that hope alive.

The free peoples of the world look to us for support in maintaining their freedoms.

If we falter in our leadership, we may endanger the peace of the world—and we shall surely endanger the welfare of our own Nation.

Great responsibilities have been placed upon us by the swift movement of events.

I am confident that the Congress will face these responsibilities squarely.

A Foreign Policy for Americans (1951)*

Robert A. Taft

Robert Alfonso Taft, son of President William Howard Taft, was United States Senator from Ohio, 1939–1953. Known and respected as Mr. Republican during the Franklin Roosevelt–Harry Truman administrations, he was an important critic of foreign policies that he believed went dangerously beyond their overriding purpose of maintaining liberty and peace at home.

I do not believe it is a selfish goal for us to insist that the overriding purpose of all American foreign policy should be the maintenance of the liberty and the peace of the people of the United States so that they may achieve that intellectual and material improvement which is their genius and in which they can set an example for all peoples. By that example we can do an even greater service to mankind than we can by billions of material assistance—and more than we can ever do by war.

Just as our nation can be destroyed by war it can also be destroyed by a political or economic policy at home which destroys liberty or breaks down the fiscal and economic structure of the United States. We cannot adopt a foreign policy which gives away all of our people's earnings or imposes such a tremendous burden on the individual American as, in effect, to destroy his incentive and his ability to increase production and productivity and his standard of living. We cannot assume a financial burden in our foreign policy so great that it threatens liberty at home.

It follows that except as such policies may ultimately protect our own security, we have no primary interest as a national policy to improve conditions or material welfare in other parts of the world or to change other forms of government. Certainly we should not engage in war to achieve such purposes. I don't mean to say that, as responsible citizens of the world, we should not gladly extend charity or assistance to those in need. I do not mean to say that we should

*From *A Foreign Policy for Americans* by Robert A. Taft. Copyright 1951 by Robert A. Taft. Reprinted by permission of Doubleday & Company, Inc.

not align ourselves with the advocates of freedom everywhere. We did this kind of thing for many years, and we were respected as the most disinterested and charitable nation in the world.

But the contribution of supplies to meet extraordinary droughts or famine or refugee problems or other emergencies is very different from a global plan for general free assistance to all mankind on an organized scale as part of our foreign policy. Such a plan, as carried out today, can only be justified on a temporary basis as part of the battle against communism, to prevent communism from taking over more of the world and becoming a still more dangerous threat to our security. It has been undertaken as an emergency measure. Our foreign policy in ordinary times should not be primarily inspired by the motive of raising the standard of living of millions throughout the world, because that is utterly beyond our capacity. I believe it is impossible with American money, or other outside aid, to raise in any substantial degree the standard of living of the millions throughout the world who have created their own problems of soil destruction or overpopulation. Fundamentally, I doubt if the standard of living of any people can be successfully raised to any appreciable degree except by their own efforts. We can advise; we can assist, if the initiative and the desire and the energy to improve themselves is present. But our assistance cannot be a principal motive for foreign policy or a justification for going to war.

We hear a great deal of argument that if we do not deliberately, as part of a world welfare program, contribute to the raising of standards of living of peoples with low income they will turn Communist and go to war against us. Apart from such emergency situations as justified the Marshall Plan, following World War II, I see no evidence that this is true. Recent wars have not been started by poverty-stricken peoples, as in China or India, but by prosperous peoples, as in a Germany led by dictators. The standard of living of China or India could be tripled and yet would still be so far below the United States that the Communists could play with equal force on the comparative hardships the people were suffering. Communism is stronger today in France and Italy than in India, though the standard of living and distribution is infinitely better in the first two countries.

However, I think as a general incident to our policy of protecting the peace and liberty of the people of the United States it is most important that we prevent the building up of any great resentment against the success and the wealth which we have achieved. In other words, I believe that our international trade relations should be scrupulously fair and generous and should make it clear to the other peoples of the world that we intend to be fair and generous.

For the same reason, and as a contribution to world economic progress, I believe that some program like the Point Four program is justified to a limited extent, even if the Russian threat were completely removed. I suppose the general project of a loan to Brazil to enable that country to build up a steel industry to use the natural resources which are available there [was justified]. I believe that the policy not only assisted in the development of that country in some degree but that in the long run it contributed to the growth of trade between Brazil and the United States and therefore to our own success in that field. But such programs should be sound economic projects, for the most part undertaken by private enterprise. Any United States government contribution is in the nature of charity to poor countries and should be limited in amount. We make no such contribution to similar projects in the United States. It seems to me that we should not undertake any such project in such a way as to make it a global plan for sending Americans all over the world in unlimited number to find projects upon which American money can be spent. We ought only to receive with sympathy any application from these nations and give it fair consideration.

Nor do I believe we can justify war by our natural desire to bring freedom to others throughout the world, although it is perfectly proper to encourage and promote freedom. In 1941 President Roosevelt announced that we were going to establish a moral order throughout the world: freedom of speech and expression, "everywhere in the world"; freedom to worship God "everywhere in the world"; freedom from want, and freedom from fear "everywhere in the world." I pointed out then that the forcing of any special brand of freedom and democracy on a people, whether they want it or not, by the brute force of war will be a denial of those very democratic principles which we are striving to advance.

The impracticability of such a battle was certainly shown by the progress of World War II. We were forced into an alliance with Communist Russia. I said on June 25, 1941, "To spread the four freedoms throughout the world we will ship airplanes and tanks and guns to Communist Russia. If, through our aid, Stalin is continued in power, do you suppose he will spread the four freedoms through

Finland and Estonia and Latvia and Lithuania? Do you suppose that anybody in Russia itself will ever hear of the four freedoms after the war?" Certainly if World War II was undertaken to spread freedom throughout the world it was a failure. As a matter of fact, Franklin Roosevelt never dared to go to war for that purpose, and we only went to war when our own security was attacked at Pearl Harbor.

There are a good many Americans who talk about an American century in which America will dominate the world. They rightly point out that the United States is so powerful today that we should assume a moral leadership in the world to solve all the troubles of mankind. I quite agree that we need that moral leadership not only abroad but also at home. We can take the moral leadership in trying to improve the international organization for peace. I think we can take leadership in the providing of example and advice for the improvement of material standards of living throughout the world. Above all, I think we can take the leadership in proclaiming the doctrines of liberty and justice and impressing on the world that only through liberty and law and justice, and not through socialism or communism, can the world hope to obtain the standards which we have attained in the United States. Our leaders can at least stop apologizing for the American system, as they have been apologizing for the past fifteen years. . . .

The trouble with those who advocate this policy is that they really do not confine themselves to moral leadership. . . . In their hearts they want to force on these foreign peoples through the use of American money and even, perhaps, American arms the policies which moral leadership is able to advance only through the sound strength of its principles and the force of its persuasion. I do not think this moral leadership ideal justifies our engaging in any preventive war, or going to the defense of one country against another, or getting ourselves into a vulnerable fiscal and economic position at home which may invite war. I do not believe any policy which has behind it the threat of military force is justified as part of the basic foreign policy of the United States except to defend the liberty of our own people.

In order to justify a lend-lease policy or the Atlantic Pact program for mutual aid and for arming Europe in time of peace or the Marshall Plan or the Point Four program beyond a selective and limited extent, any such program must be related to the liberty of the United States. Our active partisanship in World War II was based on the theory that a Hitler victory would make Germany a serious threat to the liberty of the United States. I did not believe that Germany would be such a threat, particularly after Hitler brought Russia into the war, and that is the reason I opposed the war policy of the Administration from the elections of 1940 to the attack on the United States at Pearl Harbor in December 1941. The more recent measures for Marshall Plan aid on a global scale—and to the extent of billions of dollars of American taxpayers' money—and the Atlantic Pact arms program are and must be based on the theory that Russia today presents a real threat to the security of the United States.

While I may differ on the extent of some of these measures, I agree that there is such a threat. This is due principally to the facts that air power has made distances so short and the atomic bomb has made air power so potentially effective that Russia today could do what Hitler never could do—inflict serious and perhaps crippling injury on our cities and on our industrial plants and the other production resources which are so essential to our victory in war.

Furthermore, the Russians combine with great military and air power a fanatical devotion to Communism not unlike that which inspired the Moslem invasion of Europe in the Middle Ages. The crusading spirit makes possible fifth-column adjunct to military attack which adds tremendously to the power and danger of Russian aggression. The Russian threat has become so serious today that in defense of the liberty and peace of the people of the United States I think we are justified in extending economic aid and military aid to many countries, but only when it can be clearly shown in each case that such aid will be an effective means of combating Communist aggression. We have now felt it necessary in order to protect the liberty of the United States against an extraordinary special threat to adopt a policy which I do not believe should be considered as part of any permanent foreign policy. We have been forced into this not only because of the power of Soviet Russia but because the United Nations has shown that it is wholly ineffective under its present charter. The new temporary policy may be outlined as follows:

1. We have had to set up a much larger armed force than we have ever had to do before in time of peace, in order to meet the Communist threat. I believe this effort should be directed particularly toward a development of an all-powerful air force.

2. We have had to adopt as a temporary measure the policy of extending economic and military aid to all those countries which, with the use of such aid, can perhaps prevent the extension of Russian military power or Russian or Communist influence. We have backed that up by announcing definitely to Russia that if it undertakes aggression against certain countries whose independence is important to us it will find itself at war with us. This is a kind of Monroe Doctrine for Europe.

3. We have had to adopt a policy of military alliances to deter, at least, the spread of Communist power. To control sea and air throughout the world, the British alliance is peculiarly important. Again, we hope that with the decline of Russian power and the re-establishment of an international organization for peace such alliances may be unnecessary.

I opposed that feature of the Atlantic Pact which looked toward a commitment of the United States to fight a land war on the continent of Europe and therefore opposed, except to a limited degree, the commitment of land troops to Europe. Except as we find it absolutely essential to our security, I do not believe we should depart from the principle of maintaining a free hand to fight a war which may be forced upon us, in such a manner and in such places as are best suited at the time to meet those conditions which are changing so rapidly in the modern world. Nothing is so dangerous as to commit the United States to a course which is beyond its capacity to perform with success.

Honolulu Declaration (1966)

Issued by President Lyndon B. Johnson and the South Vietnamese Chief of State, Lieut. Gen. Nguyen Van Thieu, and Premier Nguyen Cao Ky, on February 8, 1966.

Declaration of Honolulu

Part I.

The Republic of Vietnam and the United States of America jointly declare: their determination in defense against aggression, their dedication to the hopes of all the people of South Vietnam and their commitments to the search for just and stable peace.

In pursuit of these objectives the leaders of their Governments have agreed upon this declaration, which sets forth:

The purposes of the Government of Vietnam,

The purposes of the Government of the United States,

And the common commitment of both Governments.

Part II. The Purposes of the Government of Vietnam.

Here in the mid-Pacific, halfway between Asia and North America, we take the opportunity to state again the aims of our Government. We are a Government—indeed a generation—of revolutionary transformation. Our people are caught up in a mortal struggle. This struggle has four sides.

(1)

We must defeat the Vietcong and those illegally fighting with them on our soil. We are the victims of an aggression directed and supported from Hanoi. That aggression—that so-called "war of national liberation"—is part of the Communist plan for the conquest of all of Southeast Asia. The defeat of that aggression is vital for the future of our people of South Vietnam.

(2)

We are dedicated to the eradication of social injustice among our people. We must bring about a true social revolution and construct a modern society in which every man can know that he has a future; that he has respect and dignity; that he has the opportunity for himself and for his children to live in an environment where all is not disappointment, despair and dejection; that the opportunities exist for the full expression of his talents and his hopes.

(3)

We must establish and maintain a stable, viable economy and build a better material life for our people. In spite of the war, which creates many unusual and unpredictable economic situations, we are determined to continue with a policy of austerity; to make the best possible use of the assistance granted us from abroad; and to help our people achieve regular economic growth and improved material welfare.

(4)

We must build true democracy for our land and for our people. In this effort we shall continue to imbue the people with a strong sense of national unity, a stronger commitment to civic responsibility. We shall encourage a widened and more active participation in and contribution to the building of a free, independent, strong and peaceful Vietnam. In particular, we pledge again:

To formulate a democratic constitution in the months ahead, including an electoral law.

To take that constitution to our people for discussion and modification.

To seek its ratification by secret ballot.

To create, on the basis of elections rooted in that constitution, an elected government.

These things shall be accomplished mainly with the blood, intelligence and dedication of the Vietnamese people themselves. But in this interdependent world we shall need the help of others:

To win the war of independence; to build while we fight; to reconstruct and develop our nation when terror ceases.

To those future citizens of a free, democratic South Vietnam now fighting with the Vietcong, we take this occasion to say come and join in this national revolutionary adventure:

Come safely to join us through the open-arms program.

Stop killing your brothers, sisters, their elders and their children.

Come and work through constitutional democracy to build together that life of dignity, freedom and peace those in the North would deny the people of Vietnam.

Thus, we are fighting this war. It is a military war, a war for the hearts of our people. We cannot win one without winning the other. But the war for the hearts of the people is more than a military tactic. It is a moral principle. For this we shall strive as we fight to bring about a true social revolution.

Part III. The Purposes of the Government of the United States.

(1)

The United States of America is joined with the people and Government of Vietnam to prevent aggression. This is the purpose of the determined effort of the American armed forces now engaged in Vietnam. The United States seeks no bases. It seeks no colonial presence. It seeks to impose no alliance or alignment. It seeks only to prevent aggression, and its pledge to that purpose is firm. It aims simply to help a people and government who are determined to help themselves.

(2)

The United States is pledged to the principles of the self-determination of peoples, and of government by the consent of the governed. It therefore gives its full support to the purpose of free elections proclaimed by the Government of South Vietnam and to the principle of open arms and amnesty for all who turn from terror toward peace and rural construction. The United States will give its full support to measures of social revolution, including land reform based upon the principle of building upward from the hopes and purposes of all the people of Vietnam.

(3)

Just as the United States is pledged to play its part in the world-wide attack upon hunger, ignorance and disease, so in Vietnam it will give special support to the work of the people of that country to build even while they fight.

We have helped and we will help them—to stabilize the economy, to increase the production of food, to spread the light of education, to stamp out disease.

(4)

The purpose of the United States remains a purpose of peace. The United States Government and the Government of Vietnam will continue in the future, as they have in the past, to press the quest for a peaceful settlement in every forum. The world knows the harsh and negative response these efforts have thus far received. The world should know, too, that the United States Government and the Government of Vietnam remain determined that no path to peace shall be unexplored. Within the framework of their international commitments, the United States and Vietnam aim to create with others a stable peace in Southeast Asia which will permit the governments and peoples of the region to devote themselves to lifting the condition of man. With the understanding and support of the Government of Vietnam, the peace offensive of the United States Government and the Government of South Vietnam will continue until peace is secured.

Part IV. The Common Commitment.

The President of the United States and the chief of state and Prime Minister of the Republic of Vietnam are thus pledged again:

To defense against aggression,
To the work of social revolution,
To the goal of free self-government,
To the attack on hunger, ignorance and disease,
And to the unending quest for peace.

Chapter Five

The American Democracy as Democratization and Modernization in the New Nations

In the selections that follow, we turn to strategies of democratization and modernization among the developing nations. We may put our faith in the belief that all people naturally desire "freedom and equality," or we may choose the path of security and put our faith in firm military and economic aid and by that at least insure law and order. Neither choice has proved entirely satisfactory. Professor Almond examines these simplistic choices and suggests a way out.

Although Professor von der Mehden concedes the magic-wand effect of the fashionable word "democracy" among the new nations, he exposes key differences in purpose and emphasis among these countries and identifies and classifies the kinds of democracy springing up around the world. Students should relate the American ideas of democracy illustrated in Chapter One with the distinctions made here.

Finally, one of America's leading social philosophers, Reinhold Niebuhr, injects a warning note into the attempt to extend democracy abroad. He feels we should beware of dogmatizing democracy into a single, packaged doctrine in order to offer it to nations as the only alternative to communism. As wide apart as the two systems are, neither system can be divorced from the realities of regional development; thus neither system can be considered a convincing utopia. In any case a direct confrontation of "utopias" is the worst possible way of mediating between their competitive vitalities. It is wise to avoid fixed interpretations of history. There will be perils enough for the new nations without the burdens of messianic idealism.

Making New Nations Democratic*

Gabriel A. Almond

Professor Gabriel Almond served on the faculty of Political Science at Princeton University before joining Stanford University as chairman of the Department of Political Science. He is a leading scholar in the relatively new fields of political culture and comparative political systems.

Must It Be All Or Nothing?

There has been no end of debate in recent years on the question of political modernization and democratization in the new and modernizing nations of Asia, Africa and Latin America. One of the schools of thought goes like this. The very idea of democracy in these nations was a naive one. How can we take a delicate mechanism and subtle culture like democracy, which took centuries of groping and trial and error to develop in the West, and transplant it into societies with radically different political cultures, social structures and political traditions? What we have to settle for in the so-called developing and uncommitted world, goes this line of reasoning, are political stability and the military-strategic interests of the United States.

There have been two approaches in our appraisals of the prospects of these new and modernizing nations, a "tough" one and a "tender" one; and these have been the points of view expressed in our political debate about foreign aid and America's role in the developing and transitional world. The "tender" approach grows out of the liberal enlightenment tradition in America, the faith in man's inclination to freedom and justice, a belief in education and educability, a belief in the democratic consequences of economic progress. This school of thought imputed to the democratic constitutions which were established in Asia and Africa after World War II a reality which they could not have possessed. And as Korea, Vietnam, Burma, Indonesia, Pakistan, Egypt, Ghana, Cuba and Brazil—I won't attempt to

*Reprinted from *Stanford Today*, Series 1, No. 10 (Autumn, 1964), with the permission of the publishers, Stanford University.

name them all—have turned to authoritarian and even Communist regimes— this school of thought has become demoralized. It had no prepared ground to fall back on, and, as a consequence, has tended to play into the hands of the "tough" school of thought, tended to lend credibility to [the] point of view of simply holding the line. . . .

Two distortions of reality underlie the "tender" approach. The first is the failure to perceive accurately and without illusion the human and social material of the new nations, and the complexity of the institutions we were expecting them to operate. I shall return to this problem at a later point. The second is our failure to appreciate how recent and how partial is our own attainment of democracy in the West. Not much more than a century ago England, the mother of parliaments, looked very much like one of our non-Western nations. It had a serious problem of illiteracy, or of low literacy, a working class living in rude poverty, a small aristocratic elite based substantially on landed property monopolizing political power. In contemporary England the old society is only slowly giving way to pressures for equalizing opportunity, and there is a good long way to go. In our own United States the denial of equal opportunities on grounds of race is still a popular policy among the great majority of Southern whites and a large, a very large minority of Northern whites. Two of the great European powers, Italy and Germany, not long ago explicitly rejected democratic processes, and Germany left memories of destructiveness and barbarism which all human history will be unable to wipe out. France, of the glorious revolutionary tradition, now lives in a state of suspended democracy by popular request, so to speak, because of the long and humiliating failures of her republican regimes.

I stress these points only to remind ourselves that we are not comparing an exotic, backward, chaotic and authoritarian world with a modern democratic one, but rather for both the old and the new nations we are dealing with an unfulfilled process of enlightenment and democratization. This should reduce our impatience and panic at the excesses and instabilities of the new nations. . . .

What I have called the "tough" approach is also based on a number of myths and false expectations. One of these is that stable, military and conservative regimes are really stable. We need only recall the events of recent years and months in South Korea, in Vietnam, pre-Castro Cuba, or Brazil. The forces which are alive in the world today are too powerful to be contained for long. What looks like stability and viability today may end in an Iraqian blood bath tomorrow. Surely we may have to support such regimes, but we cannot rest our policy of support on the theory that their stability is more than superficial. In addition there is a tendency for extremism to breed extremism, repression, repression. It may very well be that these repressive regimes are the ones most susceptible to Communist penetration like the Cuba of Batista, that the illusion of security and stability in these areas may really be doubly illusory, so to speak.

A second myth which underlies the approach which would put our bets—and primarily military bets—on military and authoritarian regimes is what I call the dominoes theory of international politics. This theory is a very simple one. For example, it was argued when China fell to the Communists in 1949 that it would simply be a matter of time—and not much time at that—before Korea, Indo-China, Thailand, and the rest of Southeast Asia and then India would fall to the Communists. The same argument has been advanced in relation to Laos and Vietnam, and it has been said that unless the Castro regime is overturned, the rest of Latin America cannot be held.

The Chinese collapse was an immensely costly one in a strategic and political sense. A collapse of the present situation in Laos should be prevented if possible; we cannot withdraw from our present situation in Vietnam without serious risks and costs; and Cuba is a threat of major proportions. But the trouble with the dominoes theory is that it is a tense and rigid—a crisis-oriented—policy. It tends to move us from crisis to crisis, tempts us to commit our reserves prematurely. It is a panicky, defensive posture. In the long pull of foreign policy we have to be prepared to lose a position here and there, and gain some as well. We need to be deployed in depth, and husband our reserves.

We have long since passed beyond the clarities and simplicities of the cold war era and the containment policy. The Communist camp is no longer a camp, an orbit, or a bloc. It is a complex system in which the increasingly sharp struggle between Russia and China has granted a larger and larger autonomy to the smaller Communist powers and Communist parties. . . . On the Western side, the old conditions which produced NATO and the Marshall Plan have long since disappeared. Europe is economically vigorous and increasingly independent. In other words, the old unities and simplicities of the cold war are no longer with us. The structure has become loose, less predictable.

We have to revise our conceptions and strategies regarding the political prospects of the new nations in accordance with these fundamental changes in the international political system. In our relations with these nations in Asia, Africa and Latin America we are encountering the conflicting diplomacies not only of the French, the British, the Portuguese, but also the conflicting diplomacies of Russia and China. And it may very well be that the competition between Russia and China in the new nations is as hostile and antagonistic as is the Russian antagonism toward us. In this more loosely structured international political system with more competitors and a lower level of competitive intensity, we need another way of thinking about the developing nations.

Can It Happen All At Once?

We need an orderly and realistic way of fostering the process of modernization and democratization—to develop more effective policies not only for ourselves, but also for the leaders and statesmen of the new nations. Most of these men—these U Nus, Nyereres, Bandas, Mboyas, Nkrumahs, Sukarnos—have been strongly influenced by democratic ideology. The democratic political theory of the West—unlike Marxist theory—did not provide them with a theory of political growth which might help them develop sound strategies of how to move from traditional and authoritarian social and political structures toward the orderly freedoms and restraints of the democratic polity. What we need, in other words, is a good theory of *democratization,* rather than an ideological theory of democracy. The collapse of the formal democracies of Asia, Africa and Latin America might have been avoided in some cases, or at least their demoralizing consequences mitigated, had they begun with this kind of developmental conception of democratization.

What would this theory of democratization look like? In the first place it would be a theory of social change in which economic, social, psychological and political factors would have to be considered in their interrelations. It would avoid the assumptions made by economists that industrialization in and of itself brings about the development of democratic institutions. It would avoid the assumptions of lawyers and public administrators, who tend to overlook the human and social material which they sought to contain in the constitutional and administrative "bottles" of the West.

It would have to start from the vantage point of the leaderships of the new nations themselves—recognizing the resources available to them and the varieties and intensities of the pressures to which they are exposed. The statesmen of the Anglo–American West as they developed the institutions of law and popular control in the last few hundred years had a luxury of time. First, they had luxury of time to form nations out of smaller units, and patriots out of tribesmen and villagers. Second, they had a luxury of time to create governmental authority and habits of obedience to law among their populations. Third, they had a luxury of time to turn subjects into citizens as the culture and infrastructure of democracy emerged; as the suffrage expanded, the political parties, interest groups and mass media developed. And fourth, they had time to meet the demands for popular welfare that became pressing in the course of the nineteenth and twentieth centuries. The statesmen of the new and modernizing nations are hit by all of these problems at once. They confront *simultaneous* and *cumulative* revolutions. They have to make choices which Western statesmen were never called on to make.

I don't wish to give the impression that all the modernizing nations of Asia, Africa and Latin America confront these same problems in the same way and extent. But let me put it in its extreme version, taking perhaps as our model the problem which confronts Julius Nyerere of what was Tanganyika yesterday [and is Tanzania today]. He is confronted with what we may call the four problems of democratic nation-building. In the first place he has the job of creating Tanganyikans out of members of more than a hundred different tribal stocks; without this he has no nation. He has to create a framework of bureaucratic authority, dealing with a population which in its overwhelming majority consists of simple and illiterate tribesmen and villagers. He has to create citizen-participants out of this same human material, give them the right to vote before they can read, before they properly know what government is. And as he strives to raise the level of literacy and exposes his people to the amenities and physical good of modern civilization, he has somehow to respond to the growing demands for physical goods and welfare.

He confronts, in other words, a *national* revolution, an *authority* revolution, a *participation* revolution and a *welfare* revolution all at one time. It goes without saying that he cannot give in all four directions at once. Furthermore, it should also be unambiguously clear that he is not even free to choose the particular mix of revolutions or the order which he prefers. Whether he likes it or not he must give a higher priority to the creation of a nation and of effective government authority before he gives way fully to demands for participation and welfare. Indeed we may say that he must first create a nation and effective governmental authority if he is ever going to be able to respond to demands for political participation and welfare.

What this means is that whatever names we may give to them, or whatever their constitutional or legal form may be, the political systems of the new and modernizing nations will have to have strong centralizing and authoritarian tendencies. But this is not the same thing as saying we must give up the prospect of democracy in the new nations. What can be done is to build into these centralizing and authoritarian systems a democratizing strategy and pattern of investment.*

A Whig Approach To Democratization

We might call this approach to the problem of democratization the Whig approach, because it represents an effort to apply to the political development of the new nations the lessons of Western experience. As the British monarchy moved toward centralization in the fifteenth-to-seventeenth centuries, the so-called Age of Absolutism, British centralization stopped short of destroying its local autonomies—the local powers of the aristocracy and the country gentry, the self-governing rights of cities, merchant guilds and the like. A vigorous tradition of autonomy remained, fought the centralizing crown to a standstill, and preserved a traditional pluralism until a modern one was ready to combine with it in the nineteenth and twentieth centuries. It was the chaffering and bargaining of spokesmen of the crown with Whig aristocrats and middle-class merchants in Parliament which created the culture of the parliamentary bargaining and discussion, which enabled Britain to pass

*See Myron Weiner, "Political Modernization and Evolutionary Theory," in Herbert R. Barringer, George Blanksten, and Raymond Mack, eds., *Social Change in Developing Areas* (Cambridge, Mass.: Schenkman, 1965).

through the later crises of industrialization with a minimum of violence and discontinuity, relying on electoral and parliamentary processes. On the other hand you will recall from political history that the destruction of local and pluralistic tendencies in France and the extreme centralization which took place in that country are often used as an explanation of the instability of republican and democratic processes in France.

But is the Whig theory applicable in the new nations? Does it apply in India, Burma, Indonesia, Nigeria, Kenya and Uganda, [Tanzania] and the like? The answer must be, it applies in some areas more than in others. It depends in part on the vigor of local and parochial institutions, the tribal structure and the religious composition. And it also depends on what happened in the colonial period or in the earlier history of these nations. It has a more obvious relevance to India with its strong local cultural traditions, Nigeria with its strong and well-balanced tribal structure, perhaps in Kenya and Uganda and other countries with similar structures. But even in those nations without vigorous local structures and traditions—the Whig theory has some important lessons for us. It suggests a moderate form of authoritarianism, a kind of tutelary authoritarianism (such as that of Nyerere . . . , or the pattern of the Mexican revolution), a moderate pattern of penetration and centralization in which resisting groups are not destroyed, but bargained with, and occasionally conceded to, even at some cost in efficiency.

If the centralizing tendencies in these first two phases of political development—the creation of national identity and effective government—stop short of destroying local initiative, but assimilate them into a bargaining process, then the democratizing processes of education and mass communication, industrialization, urbanization and the emancipation of women can build on this pluralism and something like a viable democratic process may in time emerge. At least some of the new nations may be able to move continuously and incrementally into modernization and democratization, preserving and assimilating the pluralisms of the traditional society until the pluralism of the industrial society can emerge.

There will be many failures. We cannot properly sit in judgment of those leaders who, confronted with this cumulative revolutionary process, decide to concentrate their resources on economic development, who suppress disruptive movements, or fail to cultivate democratic tendencies. Western statesmen have never been called upon to cope with such a range of issues and choices all at once. Our own foreign policy and foreign aid programs can make a significant contribution in this modernizing and democratizing process by increasing the scale of resources available to the leaders of these nations, and by making knowledge, insight, and technical know-how into the modernizing process available. But we have to be prepared to accept failures, and waste. The world around us will not collapse into Communism like a row of dominoes, nor will it transform itself in a brief few years into a community of democratic and peaceful nations.

A while back we often heard the boast from Moscow, "We will bury you," and from our side some of us would reply, "No, we will bury you." If I am not mistaken, we don't hear this particular boast from Moscow these days, particularly since the Cuban missiles crisis. I don't think either side is going to bury the other in an ideological sense. There are loosening and pluralistic tendencies at work in the Soviet Union and in other Communist nations. These are the consequence of the unremitting pressures of an increasingly educated, technically skilled and economically well-off population—pressures for privacy, pressures for dignity, pressures for professional, artistic and intellectual integrity, and for participation in decisions affecting their lives. These pressures will not bring about a free society with a multi-party system—but surely it will be a great deal looser than it is today.

Among the Western nations there is good reason for encouragement. The processes of democratization are slowly but surely at work. The status system of England is being eroded away through the spread of educational opportunity. The racial-caste system of America is under very sharp attack. It will give way slowly; there will be setbacks; but change is irresistibly on the move here. And in the new and modernizing nations of Asia, Africa and Latin America the processes of enlightenment and democratization will have their inevitable way.

The rude shocks of two world wars and the political horrors of the interwar period shook the enlightenment faith of many of us. I must confess that I am not a political relativist any more, though I flirted with this point of view . . . in the dark periods of the last decades. Who would want to deny that man is engaged in a long-run effort at attaining control over nature and of himself, and that liberty and responsibility are at the very center of his search, and this despite the distortions and caricatures that we often produce? The early enlightenment fathers were somewhat naive and impatient. It will be a longer and costlier struggle than they anticipated, and the problems are a good deal less tractable than they supposed. But the vision was sound, and the confidence well-founded.

Ideology in Developing Nations*

Fred R. von der Mehden

Professor von der Mehden of the Political Science faculty of the University of Wisconsin is a specialist in problems of the developing nations.

In categorizing ideologies, it is necessary to make divisions on several levels. An analysis made on the basis of only one facet—say, the type of secular political system considered "best"—may neglect other important elements. The initial division is made on the basis of the overall secular political-economic system which governs the relationship between citizen and state. Five somewhat arbitrary categories, with illustrative examples, follow:

1. Individualist democracy
   - Philippines
   - Malaysia
   - Liberia
2. Collective democracy
   - India
   - Cambodia
   - Former French African colonies
   - Ghana
   - Mexico
3. Proletarian democracy
   - Communist countries
4. Guided democracy
   - Burma
   - Pakistan
   - Indonesian
   - Egypt
5. Elitist
   - Saudi Arabia
   - Ethiopia

*From Fred R. von der Mehden, *Politics of the Developing Nations*, copyright 1964; reprinted by permission of the publisher, Prentice–Hall, Inc., Englewood Cliffs, New Jersey.

One preliminary generalization can be made: it is an obvious fact of political life in the postwar world that it is almost mandatory to profess an ultimate belief in democracy. Definitions of democracy and timing may differ, but the ideologies of almost all countries proclaim some sort of democratic system as the ultimate goal.

The variety of interpretations of democracy assembled below provide a fascinating example of how a term acceptable to almost all peoples may lead to misunderstanding through differences in use.

> Regarding our own democracy, I initiated the idea, calling on the people to join to fight the diseases that were the results of free-fight liberalism. I called on the people to destroy free-fight liberalism completely, and to change it into Indonesian democracy, guided democracy, or democracy with leadership.
>
> SUKARNO of Indonesia

> I would agree with my friend Julius Nyerere of Tanganyika . . . that the test of a democratic regime might not necessarily be the actual presence of a second party, or several parties, so much as whether or not the regime tolerated individuals. . . .
>
> OLYMPIO of Togo

> The denial of fundamental human rights, the destruction of the rule of law, and the suppression of opposition have been brilliantly and felicitously rationalized. The outrageous declaration of an African leader that a one-party system is in accord with the democratic way of life has been ably defended by these spokesmen of the Western democracies.
>
> AWOLOWO of Nigeria

> . . . if there is any part of the world in which, if not democratic government in the Western sense but to use a phrase of Karl Popper's "open societies" or "open government" are possible, it is West Africa.
>
> AYO OGUN.HEYE of Nigeria

> Broadly speaking, the African parliamentarian does not understand the meaning or function of the opposition. . . . He tends to regard the opposition as a saboteur who should be hounded out of the political arena.
>
> CHIEF DAVIES of Nigeria

The state system—joint dictatorship of all revolutionary classes. The political structure—democratic centralism. This is New Democratic government; this is a republic of New Democracy.

MAO TSE-TUNG of China

We must . . . have a democracy. . . . To my mind there are four prerequisites for the success of any democratic system in a country like Pakistan:

1. It should be simple to understand, easy to work, and cheap to sustain.
2. It should put to the voter only such questions as he can answer in the light of his own personal knowledge and understanding, without external prompting.
3. It should insure the effective participation of all citizens in the affairs of the country up to the level of their mental horizon and intellectual caliber.
4. It should be able to produce reasonably strong and stable governments.

AYUB KHAN of Pakistan

The Democracy for which we rose in revolt on July 23 [1952] is a peaceful, clean democracy. . . . Its purpose is freedom of the individual, freedom of livelihood, true justice—individual freedom, collective freedom, a sound socialist society. . . . This is how we understand democracy.

NASSER of Egypt

A democracy is that form of government in which the majority runs things, where the majority means something, and the interests of that majority are protected; a democracy is that in which a man is assured of all his rights, not only the right to think freely, but also the right to know how to think. . . . A real democracy . . . in which not only the majority's rights prevail, but loaded weapons are handed to that majority!

CASTRO of Cuba

We do not conceive of democracy as simply a formal cover for an unjust social order. Hence, together with the guarantee of civil liberties to all Venezuelans, we propose the redistribution of national income . . . in a form that will make the economic misery of the majority of the people and social injustice disappear from the Venezuelan scene.

BETANCOURT of Venezuela

I consider the people who constitute a society or nation as the source of all authority in that nation; as free to transact their common concerns by any agent they think proper; to change these agents individually or the organization of them in form or function whenever they please.

JEFFERSON of the United States

1. *Individualist Democracy.*

States in this category term themselves *democracies* and support economic and political individualism; thus it differs from Category 2, which might better be described as "social democratic." Two of the most prominent examples of Afro–Asian states with individualist democratic ideologies—Liberia and the Philippines—are both American–influenced, and have both developed relatively well-to-do economic-political elites with a stake in a semicapitalist ideology. Even in these states, however, the leaders do not speak in terms of stark individualism but in terms of the more socialized democracy now practiced in the United States.

Malaysia and the Philippines present an ideology more heavily private-enterprise conscious than even that of the United States. Emphasizing the necessity for establishing a "property-owning democracy," the ruling Alliance Party of Malaysia is less prone to support social welfare doctrines than the United States government is. In fact, Malaysian leaders often deny that their policies are based upon any ideology whatsoever. In the words of one politician:

> The Alliance Party, fortunately, has not tied itself up too much with ideology. To do so would have meant becoming dogmatic. Dogmatism is not good. Often dogmatism sacrifices pragmatism (practicalism). A combination of the two is preferable.[1]

Those states with nonsocialist ideologies appear to have several factors in common: their colonial experiences have not been such as to engender an emotional antiforeign attitude; the indigenous leadership is largely composed of the economic elite; and the economy of the nation has been relatively stable, thus staving off government control and strong opposition from political groups supporting

[1] *Malay Mail* (August 29, 1960).

other ideologies. This combination of factors is not common in the Afro–Asian world.

2. *Collective Democracy.*

Few of the emergent systems have not emphasized socialism as the necessary means of economic development and a natural concomitant to political democracy. Marxism in one form or another has had a tremendous impact on the thinking of Afro–Asian leaders. There is little acceptance of class war, democratic centralism, or other dogmatic elements of Marxism, but most would echo the words of the Burmese Revolutionary Council when it described "Our Belief":

> The Revolutionary Council of the Union of Burma does not believe that man will be set free from social evils as long as pernicious economic systems exist in which man exploits man and lives on the fat of such expropriation. The Council believes it to be possible only when exploitation of man by man is brought to an end and a socialist economy based on justice is established, only then can all people, irrespective of race or religion be emancipated from all social evils and set free from anxieties over food, clothing, and shelter and from inability to resist evil, for an empty stomach is not conducive to wholesome morality. . . .[2]

A number of countries cannot be described as purely individualist or collective; their policies either stress a mixed economy or are in a state of change. It is not difficult to understand the interest in socialist doctrines: the paucity of developed resources and the lack of domestic capital makes capitalism appear questionable to political leaders, who present as evidence low per capita national income and foreign ownership of existing capital. This, they argue, leads to insufficient private capital accumulation. Thus, the state must take over the process of economic development. To the Afro–Asian socialist, Marxism appears to have a close relationship to the objective conditions of his world, although not to those of the West, where the rising standards of living have cut much of the ground out from under its theoretical foundation.

---

[2] *The Burmese Way to Socialism* (Government of the Union of Burma, 1962), p. 1.

This type of thinking is buttressed by historical and environmental factors in the Afro–Asian world. Imperialism and capitalism have often been equated by nationalists desirous of eliminating all vestiges of foreign control. This antipathy is usually directed against foreign rather than domestic capital (often because the latter helps to finance the nationalistic movements). This frequently emotional anti-imperialism-anti-capitalism may lead to postindependence laws and conditions designed to discourage foreign investors, resulting in an even greater dependence on hard-pressed domestic capital. Second, the colonial administration was usually paternalistic, controlling the economy in a manner less than conducive to free enterprise. Often, the administration owned transportation and communication media, set controls on exports, rigidly limited investment by other European nations, and—in general—established an environment which made state control after independence appear natural. Paradoxically, then, the capitalist colonial states prepared the way for the socialist ideologies that now prevail in their former colonies.

Some mention should also be made of the training of and influences on the nationalist leaders. Those who went abroad were often drawn to socialist groups, in part because of the greater interest in nationalist movements shown by left-wing organizations. Communists, Fabians, and socialists of all kinds greatly influenced the Afro–Asian student. Even those leaders who remained at home fell under the spell of the writings of various Marxists who damned imperialism and capitalism and appeared to provide a simple and easily understood theory to explain the relative poverty and social underdevelopment of Afro–Asia. Comparatively few nationalist leaders were unaffected by this thinking, and only after they had won control of their countries did their book-learned ideologies begin to require some serious revision. Still, socialism in its less doctrinaire form, vaguely calling for state action for the general welfare, has remained a simple ideology, easily understood by the masses. Finally, the postwar period has found the nations of Afro–Asia in a hurry, and socialism is considered a quicker road to economic development than capitalism is. Of course, the problem is that where national resources are few, as in Chad and Niger, or mismanaged as in Indonesia, no ideology is—in itself—going to bring the promised land.

3. *Proletarian Democracy.*

This comprises all shades of Communist ideology—Titoist, Trotskyist, Stalinist, Maoist, and so on. It also speaks in the name of both democracy and socialism, and often only the trained Marxist semanticist can discover the difference in the words used by both the Communists and the social democrats. The meaning is usually quite different, but the words themselves are not. When the Communists are in one of their united front phases, the words are even more similar—and for good reason.

Many of the same reasons which have brought individuals to support social democracy have been responsible for the further leftward turn to Communism. However, three factors need greater emphasis in the Communist case. First, the existence of the Soviet Union and Communist China as anticolonialist powers assures the Afro–Asian Communist outside support as well as a strong propaganda tool (European socialists have been disappointing to the more radical independence-minded nationalists). Also, the strong centralized organization of local Communist parties provides leadership and security to individuals disorganized by the changing societies of the developing world. It also allows the Communists to direct their ideas and policies more efficiently than other parties can. Perhaps most important, Communism appears to offer quick solutions to the individual or nation desiring to get ahead in a hurry. The totalitarian methods of communism seem quicker than the give-and-take methods of democracy. It should be pointed out, however, that undiluted Communism appears to have gained comparatively few adherents in the Afro–Asian world. There is no legal Communist party in Africa and very few Communists, in spite of cries of anguish from many Western commentators. In the Middle East, only Israel allows a legal Communist party to exist. Where it has been successful in the Far East, Communism has hidden behind nationalism and what is called the two-stage revolution (the promise of initial tolerance to economic, social, and political groups, thus lulling possible opposition). Today, even those Communist parties supporting China in the Sino–Soviet dispute deny the validity of the commune system for their countries. Thus, where Communism has been victorious, it has depended upon nationalism and the unfulfilled promise of democratic tolerance, both (according to Communist ideology) facets of "decadent" Western democracy.

4. *Guided Democracy.*

This catch-all category includes those concepts which, while denying the possibilities of democracy today, promise some type of democratic system in the future. The "democratic system," when defined, is usually not envisioned as a parliamentary government but as a limited democracy with strong leadership. There is little agreement as to the vehicle of transition, although in most areas the military plays a prominent role (Pakistan, Burma, Turkey, and others). In rare cases, this ideology is expressed by the civilian leader as, for example, Sukarno. One of the classic theories of this development toward future "democracy" was that of Sun Yat-sen, early revolutionary hero of Republican China, who envisioned three stages leading to a limited democracy. The best-articulated recent example of such a theory has been the "basic democracies" system of Ayub Khan of Pakistan, which is asserted to be a means of achieving democracy through training at lower levels and indirect elections of higher councils. Other examples abound, but few have been as systematically conceived as the two cited. More often, the period of tutelage remains indefinite and the system to be established vague.

Those who propound systems of "guided democracy" vary in their rationale for this combination of guidance and democracy. A few still pay lip service to Western democratic ideals but claim that the population is in need of training and education before these can be achieved. In the same vein, military men may claim that conditions in the country are not stable enough to allow the return to or the establishment of democracy. The Burmese military in 1958–60 and the South Korean junta both argued in this fashion. More numerous are the examples of elites which deny the worth of Western democracy for their nations and which call for a combination of guidance and popular sovereignty. This sort of guided democracy may be in preparation, as in Pakistan, or in existence, as in Indonesia. Its proponents claim it to be particularly well suited to the developing world where, they state, "liberal democracy" may lead to chaos and disunity but where the mores of the postwar period demand support for some sort of democratic system.

5. *Elitist Systems.*

Few leaders betray much sympathy for Western parliamentary democracy, at least in their own countries, but—to the extent that they express any ideology in a systematic form—fewer still deny the ultimate worth of the democratic system. Those who do are normally members of right-wing minority groups such as are to be found in some parts of the Middle East, or spokesmen for traditional societies, such as Ibn Saud or the late Iman of Yemen. Category 5 then differs from the rest in that these elitists refuse to be associated, now or later, with any form of government which rests with the people. One individual or a chosen few can and should hold all power.

The Alternatives to Communism*

Reinhold Niebuhr

The Reverend Reinhold Niebuhr is Charles A. Brigg Graduate Professor of Ethics, emeritus, and Vice-President of Union Theological Seminary in New York City. He is America's most distinguished living political philosopher and theologian concerned with social ethics.

It has become a settled conviction, at least among American democratic idealists, that the contest which engulfs the political life of the whole world is between Communism and democracy.

What is Communism? It is an absurd religio-political creed, within the framework of the utopian tradition of Western culture, which erupted with the breakdown of traditional culture in seventeenth-century England, eighteenth-century France and nineteenth-century Russia. The specific content which filled this framework was prompted by the highly contingent circumstances of early European industrialism when an open society, moving too tardily,

---

*This article is reprinted by permission of the *New Republic* (October 1, 1962), copyright 1962, Harrison-Blaine of New Jersey, Inc.

had not yet proved the capacity of democracy to come to terms with the power realities of modern industry, particularly the aggravation of the disbalances of power in feudal society. Most of the subsequent history of Western democracy has refuted the Communist dogma, particularly that part of it which attributes all historic evils to the one institution of private property. It should be fairly simple to display this refutation and to prove the absurdity of the Communist claims of world redemption from exploitation, imperialism and war.

But unfortunately democratic idealism complicates this simple task by oversimplifying it. It does so by presenting democracy as a universally valid and viable system of government which we are destined to present to the world as an alternative to Communism. This interpretation tends to reduce our cause to utopian dimensions very similar to Communist utopianism. We reduce democracy to utopianism whenever we obscure the fact that it required an advanced European culture centuries (roughly from the sixteenth to the nineteenth century) to make political freedom compatible with the power realities and the collective loyalties of race, language, religion, and class; centuries to validate political freedom (by correcting the disbalances in the economic order) as an instrument of justice. If Communism obscures the triumphs of an open society, democratic idealists likewise tend to obscure the whole torturous history of that society in European culture: its early chapters of the achievement of ethnic homogeneity, its later chapters in which sufficient tolerance was established to make cultural diversity compatible with communal harmony, and its final chapter of the triumph over the power realities of modern industrialism by achieving a tolerable equilibrium of power in both the political and economic sphere. The latter development involved the right of laborers to organize and bargain collectively, thus supplementing their equal, but insufficient, political power with equal economic power. This offset the power of centralized management, which according to the Communist dogma represented the final form of evil in history. The whole of the nineteenth century was required to achieve this equilibrium. In America it was not achieved until the fourth decade of the twentieth century, when a world depression finally disturbed the complacent bourgeois ethos which had reigned supreme in politics for some sixty-five years after the close of the Civil War.

Clearly an open society is not the simple option for all peoples and cultures which our democratic idealists assume. It seems to be a combination of an ultimate ideal and a luxury which only a culturally and economically advanced community can afford. It is an ultimate ideal, since no way has been found to make irresponsible power a servant of justice. It is a luxury because only a community with an advanced cultural cohesion and a complicated system of economic mutuality and competition can master the divisive forces which exist in any community. Only such a community can establish its authority over all competitive and divisive forces—and do this without military coercion. Incidentally we might remember that our nation experienced a bloody civil war because we could not solve the slavery issue by democratic accommodation of interests, or suppress an interest which clearly violated the principles upon which the nation was founded.

. . . .

The evidence proves that democracy, as it has been elaborated in the advanced nations in the West, is simply not an option for all nations, whatever their level of cultural and economic development. Perhaps the evidence of democracy's failure should serve to modify our own Messianic claims. Perhaps we should be more modest and say only that we are trying to help people achieve the highest degree of justice and technical competence they can.

It might be wise to make prudent distinctions between reversible and irreversible experiments in community and order. The irreversible ones are those which are supported by a fixed dogma and a policy which claims omnipotence for an elite, proportioned to its claims of omniscience.

It might also be prudent to analyze more rigorously the hazards which justice (not democracy) confronts in a world in which the rapid universalization of technical ability may aggravate the injustices of traditional communities and may mean both promise and peril to primitive cultures.

In brief, we cannot compete with the Communist utopia by mounting our own utopian claims. We can only modestly admit that history is charged with emergent vitalities on all levels of culture and politics and that it is our task to keep history open for every kind of experimentation, not allowing it to be closed prematurely by an absurd and coercive dogma.

Chapter Six

The American Democracy as Inevitable in an Industrial Civilization

Our colloquy turns to the interrelationship of politics and production. Science and technology began their world revolution about the same time democratic ideas did. Free trade was natural company for the doctrines of free men and free elections. And all three concepts were disruptive of older political systems. But there has often been a conflict among these goals. Popular governments may have economic liabilities, and some governments dedicated to economic development have failed to protect political rights.

But Professors Slater and Bennis find no ultimate, irreconcilable contradiction here. For them democracy is, in fact, the political system which lends itself most readily to efficient economic organization; it is an inevitable concomitant of modern industrial production. Citing such forces as communication, consensus, influence, and simple human response, they argue persuasively that democracy is a functional necessity for national survival in the face of chronic social change. According to this thesis, even the communists must eventually soften to the necessities of technological innovation and adapt democratic institutions to their needs.

Democracy Faces a Global Dilemma*

William H. McNeill

Professor McNeill is the author of books on international cooperation, aid programs, modern Greece, and a comprehensive history of Western civilization. He is presently chairman of the Department of History at the University of Chicago.

---

*From the *New York Times Magazine* (November 17, 1963).

If our form of government is man's ideal, why are there so many dictators today?

Democratic government is a rare phenomenon in history. In ancient Greece, where the idea and practice were both invented, democratic governments retained their vigor for only about two hundred years. . . . Fifty years ago, however, sanguine liberals and fearful conservatives agreed in believing that the next step in political development would be the spread of democratic self-government to all the world. In those days, democracy seemed clearly to be the wave of the future, an inevitable accompaniment to the giant steps in industrial progress. . . .

But the world's troubled history since World War I has not borne out their expectations. Democratic regimes have not spread irresistibly. On the contrary, democratic governments set up in Eastern and Central Europe just after the war, when Wilsonianism stood at high tide, proved themselves disappointingly fragile. From the start, Fascist Italy and Communist Russia challenged the American recipe of self-determination through free elections. Later, the Depression, swiftly followed by Hitler's rise to power in Germany, seemed to reverse the direction of Europe's political evolution, until at last even France, the principal Continental stronghold of democracy, collapsed ignominiously before the Nazis.

Anglo-American victory in World War II did something to re-establish the prestige of democratic government, but Western hopes for Eastern Europe were quickly nullified by the presence of the Red Army. Our democratic idealism, therefore, tended to fasten upon the emerging nations of Asia and Africa. The disappearance of one European colonial administration after another seemed to be a massive victory for self-determination and popular sovereignty.

Yet the democratic credentials of many of the new governments that came to power in Africa and Asia were, and remain, dubious. One-man rule, validated by plebiscite or by some sort of charismatic or party leadership, is far more common than the complex balances and forbearances between parties in and out of office that are required if voters are to enjoy an effective choice between alternative leaders at election time.

More recently still, democratic—or ostensibly democratic—governments in Latin America, where democratic aspirations and vocabularies are as old as in the United States, are increasingly threatened with collapse. Nor are the democratic regimes of Europe exactly secure. The existing governments of both France and Spain came to power by extralegal military action, and what was done once can all too obviously happen again when Franco and De Gaulle disappear.

[It is] difficult for us today to recover the buoyant self-confidence felt by liberals and democrats in the era before World War I. Their faith in the future of democratic government rested on an undimmed confidence in human progress and rationality. These in turn seemed anchored securely not merely in history (which recorded some awkward periods of apparent retrogression) but in truths of philosophy and science as well. How could anyone seriously doubt that men were ready to be guided by reason now that the discovery of the scientific method allowed everyone to correct errant thoughts and theories by the impersonal canons of observation and experimental verification? Had not the science of economics already explained a wide range of human behavior in terms of a free interplay among the individuals rationally pursuing their material self-interest? As for progress, its reality seemed self-evident in an age when new inventions were swarming so marvelously into being.

In such a climate of opinion, democratic self-government appeared as the natural and inevitable political counterpart to modern science and technology. The latter were the fine fruit of human reason applied to physical nature. That same reason, directed to the problem of how best to control human nature, seemed to indicate democratic and representative government as the best of all possible solutions. Free elections and free trade together would assure the fullest realization of human satisfactions, and by offering a means to adjust collisions of interest, they would also assure gradual peaceful changes in meeting altered circumstances.

. . . .

Until 1914, optimism prevailed. It was the brutal shock of World War I that destroyed the confidence Europeans had previously felt in human rationality and progress. The war Americans entered "to make the world safe for democracy" undermined it instead.

. . . .

Men of goodwill and stubborn democratic faith usually try to escape the dilemma by suggesting that democracy cannot flourish in poverty-stricken countries. There must be economic development before sweet reason—or grateful imitation of American institutions—will establish democracy on a firm and lasting foundation. This argument has usually been used to justify our massive aid programs since 1941, and in some parts of the world, most notably in Western Europe, American economic assistance did indeed stabilize democratic regimes, just as had been hoped and expected.

In Latin America, Africa, and Southeast Asia, however, economic aid has not yet had anything like the same political results. This should come as no surprise. Economic development—roads, power grids, factories, mines, new crops and fertilizers and all the other innovations—are bound to be profoundly disruptive of traditional social relationships and customs. As economic development becomes a reality, critical political balances within the developing society are sure to be upset—and violence may often result.

In preindustrial societies, whose institutions are not attuned to rapid economic development, forced-draft planning and massive investment simply mean a deliberate disruption of whatever the traditional consensus was before the aid program started. In the short run, therefore, in all the underdeveloped parts of the world, American aid programs are far more likely to undermine government by consent than to strengthen it.

Even in the most industrialized countries, where democratic traditions may be deeply rooted, unusually rapid social change puts a perceptible strain upon the political system. Poorer countries, where democracy is likely to be a recent import and where the social changes involved in major economic development are far more sharp than anything the United States has recently experienced, can be expected to respond with correspondingly sharper political reactions. When the consensus is endangered, dictatorship becomes more likely—unless, as nearly happened in the Congo after the withdrawal of the Belgian administration, the state breaks down into competing sovereignties.

In any such situation, disciplined cliques have a tremendous advantage. When the majority is disorganized and uncertain, even very small groups may become politically decisive—as Communist parties working on the principles first enunciated by Lenin in 1903 have repeatedly demonstrated. The frequency of military *coups d'état* may be explained in the same way, for military discipline can often provide a workable, if not very flexible, political instrument when no other basis for cohesion can readily be found.

The democratic dilemma here is very real. Neither the United States nor any local upholder of democratic political processes can organize a democratic counterpart to the Communist party, or commit a military or paramilitary force to political action without betraying democratic principles. Nevertheless, there are times when majority rule simply will not work, or else will produce irresponsible and ineffective governments that hinder rather than help economic development.

It is quite unreasonable always to expect a society launched upon rapid and drastic social change to maintain a government that is both democratic and economically progressive. On many important issues, there is no majority opinion at all. On some issues—more pay for less work, for example, or "let's kick the foreigners out"—it may be possible for a demagogue to create a general consensus, but platforms of this sort are incompatible with economic development and may actually lead to a decline from levels previously achieved. This appears to have happened, for example, in both Indonesia and Cuba and it may be occurring also in parts of Africa.

The plain fact is that economic development is nearly always unpopular. Everyone wants the end result, but no one wants to undergo the necessary hardship and effort in the beginning. Even in the United States, where industrialism grew smoothly out of preexisting values and legal relationships, the robber barons and captains of industry who took the lead in amassing industrial capital were never exactly popular. Had their acts and policies been subject to democratic supervision, it is safe to say that the industrialization of the United States would have proceeded far more slowly than was in fact the case.

The problems are a little less acute when capital investment comes from abroad. Direct collision between the requirements of daily consumption and the need for capital accumulation is thereby postponed or even evaded. But a massive inflow of foreign capital, whether through private or public channels, is still going to be unpopular. Capital inflow means change, and change always hurts someone. Moreover, foreign capital is unfailingly accompanied by foreign advisers and administrators. No matter how careful they may be to respect local sensitivities, foreigners with the kind of power over local affairs that the disposal of outside capital provides will always arouse antagonism.

No genuinely democratic government can afford, therefore, to be too closely associated with foreign capital and advisers. Save in unusually propitious circumstances, a truly popular government is far more likely to *obstruct* economic development and *repudiate* foreign advice than to accept aid in a cooperative spirit. Authoritarian governments, on the other hand, have great advantages in planning and carrying through vast projects of social and industrial engineering. Their planners need not wait for popular approval.

We should recognize, therefore, that the energetic pursuit of economic development does not necessarily create the conditions for stable democratic government. Rapid change is far more likely to hatch a brood of more or less authoritarian regimes of the type that predominate today in the underdeveloped countries of the world.

Nevertheless, despite these unpalatable facts, we are not justified in jumping to the conclusion that democracy has no future in an industrialized world. Perhaps it has—perhaps it hasn't. On balance, the complex, diverse political systems of modern democracies may turn out to be better suited than monolithic authoritarianism for sustaining and maintaining industrial societies. When specialists are so specialized and so indispensable, perhaps a system of government that permits various points of view to find public expression and adjusts conflicts of interest through an open electoral process will prove to be more viable because of its flexibility.

. . . .

Hence, the rash of dictatorships with which the world is now afflicted may turn out to be a childhood disease of industrial society. Perhaps the rash will fade as the first catastrophic phase of industrialization recedes into history. Our descendants may yet live to see the day when more supple and democratic political institutions inherit the earth—just as our grandfathers so confidently expected.

No one, however, can yet be sure. Industrialism and democracy may not have any natural affinity. . . .

Democracy Is Inevitable*

Philip E. Slater and Warren G. Bennis

We praise democracy but secretly nurse the fear that it is a luxury. Assistant Professor of Sociology at Brandeis University, Philip Slater; and Professor of Industrial Management at Massachusetts Institute of Technology, Warren Bennis, think otherwise and give their reasons for its universal values, uses, and inevitability.

. . . We will argue that democracy has been so widely embraced, not because of some vague yearning for human rights, but because *under certain conditions* it is a more "efficient" form of social organization. (Our concept of efficiency includes the ability to survive and prosper.) We do not regard it as accidental that those nations of the world which have endured longest under conditions of relative wealth and stability are democratic, while authoritarian regimes have, with few exceptions, either crumbled or eked out a precarious and backward existence. . . .

Our position is, in brief, that democracy (whether capitalistic or socialistic is not at issue here) is the only system which can sucfessfully cope with the changing demands of contemporary civilization. We are not necessarily endorsing democracy as such; one might reasonably argue that industrial civilization is pernicious and should be abolished. We suggest merely that given a desire to survive in this civilization, democracy is the most effective means to achieve this end. . . .

Democracy Takes Over

There are signs, in fact, that our business community is becoming aware of this law. Several of the newest and most rapidly blooming companies in the United States boast unusually democratic

---

*From the *Harvard Business Review* (March–April, 1964), reprinted by permission of the publisher, copyright 1964 by the President and Fellows of Harvard College.

organizations. Even more surprising is the fact that some of the largest of the established corporations have been moving steadily, if accidentally, toward democratization. Frequently they began by feeling that administrative vitality and creativity were lacking in the older systems of organization. In increasing numbers, therefore, they enlisted the support of social scientists and of outside programs, the net *effect* of which has been to democratize their organization....

So far, the data are not all in; conclusive evidence is missing, but the forecast seems to hold genuine promise: that it is possible to bring about greater organizational effectiveness through the utilization of valid social knowledge.

System of Values

What we have in mind when we use the term "democracy" is not "permissiveness" or "laissez faire," but a system of values—a "climate of beliefs" governing behavior—which people are internally compelled to affirm by deeds as well as words. These values include:

1. Full and free *communication,* regardless of rank and power.

2. A reliance on *consensus,* rather than the more customary forms of coercion or compromise to manage conflict.

3. The idea that *influence* is based on technical competence and knowledge rather than on the vagaries of personal whims or prerogatives of power.

4. An atmosphere that permits and even encourages emotional *expression* as well as task-oriented acts.

5. A basically *human* bias, one that accepts the inevitability of conflict between the organization and the individual, but which is willing to cope with and mediate this conflict on rational grounds.

Changes along these dimensions are being promoted widely in American industry. Most important, for our analysis, is what we believe to be the reason for these changes: *democracy becomes a functional necessity whenever a social system is competing for survival under conditions of chronic change.*

Adaptability to Change

The most familiar variety of such change to the inhabitants of the modern world is technological innovation. This has been characterized most dramatically by J. Robert Oppenheimer.[1]

> One thing that is new is the prevalence of newness, the changing scale and scope of change itself, so that the world alters as we walk on it, so that the years of a man's life measure not some small growth or rearrangement or moderation of what he learned in childhood but a great upheaval.

But if change has now become a permanent and accelerating factor in American life, then adaptability to change becomes increasingly the most important single determinant of survival. The profit, the saving, the efficiency, the morale of the moment becomes secondary to keeping the door open for rapid readjustment to changing conditions.

Organization and communication research at the Massachusetts Institute of Technology reveals quite dramatically what type of organization is best suited for which kind of environment. Specifically:[2]

> For simple tasks under static conditions, an autocratic centralized structure, such as has characterized most industrial organizations in the past, is quicker, neater, and more efficient.
>
> But for adaptability to changing conditions, for "rapid acceptance of a new idea," for "flexibility in dealing with novel problems, generally high morale and loyalty . . . the more egalitarian or decentralized type seems to work better." One of the reasons for this is that the centralized decision-maker is "apt to discard an idea on the grounds that he is too busy or the idea too impractical."

Our argument for democracy rests on an additional factor, one that is fairly complicated but profoundly important in shaping our

---

[1]In *Perspectives USA* (Spring, 1955).

[2]W. G. Bennis in *General Systems Yearbook* (December, 1962).

ideas. First of all, it is interesting to note that modern industrial organization has been based roughly on the antiquated system of the military ... such as "line and staff," "standard operating procedure," "table of organization," and so on. . . . By and large these conceptions are changing, and even the military is moving away from the oversimplified and questionable assumptions on which its organization was originally based. . . .

This change has been coming about because of the palpable inadequacy of the military-bureaucratic model, particularly its response to rapid change; and also because the institution of science is now emerging as a more suitable model.

Scientific Attitude

But why is science gaining acceptance as a model? . . .

We believe that science is winning out because the challenges facing modern enterprises are, at base, *knowledge*-gathering, *truth*-requiring dilemmas. Managers are not scientists, nor do we expect them to be. But the processes of problem solving, conflict resolution, and recognition of dilemmas have great kinship with the academic pursuit of truth. The institution of science is the only institution based on and geared for change. It is built not only to adapt to change, but to overthrow and create change. So it is—and will be—with modern industrial enterprises.

And here we come to the point. In order for the "spirit of inquiry," the foundation of science, to grow and flourish, there is a necessity for a democratic environment. Science encourages a political view which is egalitarian, pluralistic, liberal. It accentuates freedom of opinion and dissent. It is against all forms of totalitarianism, dogma, mechanization, and blind obedience. . . .

In other words, democracy in industry is not an idealistic conception but a hard necessity in those areas in which change is ever-present and in which creative scientific enterprise must be nourished. For democracy is the only system of organization which is compatible with perpetual change.

Retarding Factors

It might be objected here that we have been living in an era of rapid technological change for a hundred years, without any noticeable change in the nature of the average industrial firm. True there are many restrictions on the power of the executive over his subordinates now compared with those prevailing at the end of the nineteenth century. But this hardly constitutes industrial democracy—the decision-making function is still an exclusive and jealously guarded prerogative of the top echelons. If democracy is an inevitable consequence of perpetual change, why then have we not seen more dramatic changes in the structure of industrial organizations? The answer is twofold.

Obsolete Individuals

First, the rate of technological change is a rapidly accelerating one. . . . We are now beginning an era when a man's knowledge and approach can become obsolete before he has even begun the career for which he was trained. The value of what one learns is always slipping away, like the value of money in a runaway inflation. We are living in an era which could be characterized as a runaway inflation of knowledge and skill, and it is this which is perhaps responsible for the feelings of futility, alienation, and lack of individual worth which are said to characterize our time.

Under such conditions, the individual *is* of relatively little significance. No matter how imaginative, energetic, and brilliant he may be, time will soon catch up with him to the point where he can profitably be replaced by someone equally imaginative, energetic, and brilliant, but with a more up-to-date viewpoint and fewer obsolete preconceptions. . . .

Powers of Resistance

The second reason is that the mere existence of a dysfunctional tendency, such as the relatively slow adaptability of authoritarian structures, does not automatically bring about its disappearance. This drawback must first either be recognized for what it is or become so severe as to destroy the structures in which it is embedded. Both of these conditions are only now beginning to make themselves felt, primarily through the peculiar nature of modern technological competition.

The crucial change has been that the threat of technological defeat no longer comes necessarily from rivals within the industry, who usually can be imitated quickly without too great a loss, but often from outside—from new industries using new materials in new ways. One can therefore make no intelligent prediction about "what the next likely development in our industry will be." The blow may come from anywhere. Correspondingly, a viable corporation cannot merely develop and advance in the usual ways. In order to survive and grow it must be prepared to *go* anywhere—to develop new products or techniques even if they are irrelevant to the present activities of the organization. It is perhaps for this reason that the beginnings of democratization have appeared most often in industries (such as electronics) which depend heavily on invention. It is undoubtedly for this reason that more and more sprawling behemoths are planning consequential changes in their organizational structures and climates toward releasing democratic potentiality.

Farewell to "Great Men"

The passing of years has also given the *coup de grace* to another force that retarded democratization—the "great man" who with brilliance and farsightedness could preside with dictatorial powers at the head of a growing organization and keep it at the vanguard of American business. In the past he was usually a man with a single idea, or a constellation of related ideas, which he developed brilliantly. This is no longer enough.

Today, just as he begins to reap the harvest of his imagination, he finds that someone else (even perhaps one of his stodgier competitors, aroused by desperation) has suddenly carried the innovation a step further, or found an entirely new and superior approach to it, and he is suddenly outmoded. How easily can he abandon his idea, which contains all his hopes, his ambitions, his very heart? His aggressiveness now begins to turn in on his own organization; and the absolutism of his position begins to be a liability, a dead hand, an iron shackle, upon the flexibility and growth of the company. But he cannot be removed—in the short run the firm would even be hurt by his loss, since its prestige derives to such an extent from his reputation. And by the time he has left, the organization will have receded into a secondary position within the industry. It may even decay further when his personal touch is lost.

The "cult of personality" still exists, of course, but it is rapidly fading. More and more large corporations (General Motors, for one) predicate their growth not on "heroes" but on solid management teams.

"Organization Men"

Taking the place of the "great men," we are often told, is the "organization man." A good many tears have been shed over this transition by liberals and conservatives alike. The liberals, of course, have in mind, as "the individual," some sort of creative deviant—an intellectual, artist, or radical politician. The conservatives are thinking of the old captains of industry and perhaps some great generals. (In the Soviet Union they think of Stalin.)

Neither is at all unhappy to lose the "individuals" mourned by the other, dismissing them contemptuously as communists and rabble-rousers, on the one hand, and criminals and facists, on the other. What is particularly confusing in terms of the present issue is a tendency to equate conformity with autocracy—to see the new industrial organization as one in which all individualism is lost except for a few villainous individualistic manipulators at the top.

But this, of course, is absurd in the long run. The trend toward the "organization man" is also a trend toward a looser and more flexible organization in which the roles are to some extent interchangeable and no one is indispensable. To many people this trend is a monstrous nightmare, but one should at least not confuse it with the nightmares of the past. It may mean anonymity and homogeneity, but it does not and cannot mean authoritarianism, in the long run, despite the bizarre anomalies and hybrids that may arise in a period of transition.

The reason it cannot is that it arises out of a need for flexibility and adaptability. Democracy and the dubious trend toward the "organization man" alike (for this trend *is* a part of democratization, whether we like this aspect of democracy or not) arise from the need to maximize the availability of appropriate knowledge, skill, and insight under conditions of great variability.

Rise of the Professional

While the "organization man" idea has titillated the imagination of the American public, it has masked a far more fundamental change now taking place: the rise of the "professional man." Professional specialists, holding advanced degrees in such abstruse sciences as cryogenics or computer logic as well as the more mundane business disciplines, are entering all types of organizations at a higher rate than any other sector of the labor market.

And these men can hardly be called "organization men." They seemingly derive their rewards from inward standards of excellence, from their professional societies, from the intrinsic satisfaction of their task. In fact, they are committed to the *task,* not the job; to their standards, not their boss. And because they have degrees, they travel. They are not good "company men"; they are uncommitted except to the challenging environments where they can "play with problems."

These new "professional men" are remarkably compatible with our conception of a democratic system. For like these "new men," democracy seeks no new stability, no end point; it is purposeless, save that it purports to ensure perpetual transition, constant alteration, ceaseless instability. It attempts to upset nothing, but only to facilitate the potential upset of anything. Democracy and our new professional men identify primarily with the adaptive process, not the "establishment."

Yet it must also be remembered that all democratic systems are not entirely so—there are always limits to the degree of fluidity which can be borne. Thus, it is not a contradiction to the theory of democracy to find that a particular democratic society or organization may be more "conservative" than some autocratic one. Indeed, the most dramatic, violent, and drastic changes have always taken place under autocratic regimes, for such changes usually require prolonged self-denial, while democracy rarely lends itself to such voluntary asceticism. But these changes have been viewed as finite and temporary, aimed at a specific set of reforms, and moving toward a new state of nonchange. It is only when the society reaches a level of technological development in which survival is dependent on the institutionalization of perpetual change that democracy becomes necessary.

Reinforcing Factors

The Soviet Union is rapidly approaching this level and is beginning to show the effects, as we shall see. The United States has already reached it. Yet democratic institutions existed in the United

States when it was still an agrarian nation. Indeed, democracy has existed in many places and at many times, long before the advent of modern technology. How can we account for these facts?

Expanding Conditions

In the first place, it must be remembered that modern technology is not the only factor which could give rise to conditions of necessary perpetual change. Any situation involving rapid and unplanned expansion, sustained over a sufficient period of time, will tend to produce great pressure for democratization. Secondly, when we speak of democracy, we are referring not only or even primarily to a particular political format. Indeed, American egalitarianism has perhaps its most important manifestation, not in the Constitution, but in the family.

Historians are fond of pointing out that Americans have always lived under expanding conditions—first the frontier, then the successive waves of immigration, now a runaway technology. The social effects of these kinds of expansion are of course profoundly different in many ways, but they share one impact in common: all have made it impossible for an authoritarian family system to develop on a large scale. Every foreign observer of American mores since the seventeenth century has commented that American children "have no respect for their parents," and every generation of Americans since 1650 has produced forgetful native moralists complaining about the decline in filial obedience and deference.

Descriptions of family life in colonial times make it quite clear that American parents were as easy-going, permissive, and child-oriented then as now, and the children as independent and "disrespectful." This "lack of respect" is, of course, not for the "parents" as individuals, but for the concept of parental authority as such.

The basis for this loss of respect has been outlined quite dramatically by historian Oscar Handlin, who points out that in each generation of early settlers, the children were more at home in their new environment than their parents—had less fear of the wilderness, fewer inhibiting European preconceptions and habits. Furthermore, their parents were heavily dependent on them physically and economically. This was less true of the older families after the East became settled. But as one moved neearer to the frontier, the conditions for familial democracy became again strikingly marked, so that the cultural norm was ever protected from serious decay.

Further reinforcement came later from new immigrants, who similarly found their children better adapted to the world than themselves, because of their better command of the language, better knowledge of the culture, better occupational opportunities, and so forth. It was the children who were expected to improve the social position of the family, and who through their exposure to peer groups and the school system could act as intermediaries between their parents and the new world. It was not so much "American ways" that shook up the old family patterns, but the demands and requirements of a new situation. How could the young look to the old as the ultimate fount of wisdom and knowledge when, in fact, that knowledge was irrelevant—when indeed the children had a better practical grasp of the realities of American life than did their elders?

The New Generation

These sources of reinforcement have now disappeared. But a third has only begun. Rapid technological change again means that the wisdom of elders is largely obsolete, and that the young are better adapted to their culture than are their parents. How many of the latter can keep up with their children in knowledge of the sciences, for example? Santayana put it beautifully when he said: "No specific hope about distant issues is ever likely to be realized. The ground shifts, the will of mankind deviates, and what the father dreamt of the children neither fulfill nor desire."[3]

It is this fact that reveals the basis for the association between democracy and change. The old, the learned, the powerful, the wealthy, those in authority—these are the ones who are committed. They have learned a pattern and succeeded in it. But when change comes, it is often the *uncommitted* who can best realize it, take advantage of it. This is why primogeniture has always lent itself so easily to social change in general and industrialization in par-

---

[3]*The Philosophy of Santayana*, edited by Irwin Edman (New York: Modern Library, Random House, 1936).

ticular. The uncommitted younger sons, barred from success in the older system, are always ready to exploit new opportunities. In Japan, these younger sons were treated more indulgently by the parents, and given more freedom to choose an occupation. . . .

Doubt and Fears

Indeed, we may even in this way account for the poor opinion which democracy has of itself. We underrate the strength of democracy because democracy creates a general attitude of doubt, of skepticism, of modesty. It is only among the authoritarian that we find the dogmatic confidence, the self-righteousness, the intolerance and cruelty that permit one never to doubt oneself and one's beliefs. The looseness, the sloppiness, and the untidiness of democratic structures express the feeling that what has been arrived at today is probably only a partial solution and may well have to be changed tomorrow.

In other words, one cannot believe that change is in itself a good thing and still believe implicitly in the rightness of the present. Judging from the report of history, democracy has always underrated itself—one cannot find a democracy anywhere without also discovering (side-by-side with expressions of outrageous chauvinism) an endless pile of contemptuous and exasperated denunciations of it. (One of the key issues in our national politics today, as in the presidential campaign in 1960, is our "national prestige.") And perhaps this is only appropriate. For when a democracy ceases finding fault with itself, it has probably ceased to be a democracy.

Overestimating Autocracy

But feeling doubt about our own social system need not lead us to overestimate the virtues and efficiency of others. We can find this kind of overestimation in the exaggerated fear of the "Red Menace"—mere exposure to which is seen as leading to automatic conversion. Few authoritarians can conceive of the possibility that an individual could encounter an authoritarian ideology and not be swept away by it.

Of a similar nature, but more widespread, is the "better dead than Red" mode of thinking. Here again we find an underlying assumption that communism is socially, economically, and ideologically inevitable—that once the military struggle is lost, all is lost. It is interesting that in all of our gloomy war speculations, there is never any mention of an American underground movement. It is everywhere assumed that if a war were fought in which anyone survived and the Soviet Union won, then:

All Americans would immediately become Communists.

The Soviet Union would set up an exact replica of itself in this country.

It would work.

The Soviet system would remain unchanged.

The Soviets in America would be uninfluenced by what they found here.

Not only are these assumptions patently ridiculous; they also reveal a profound misconception about the nature of social systems. The structure of a society is not determined merely by a belief. It cannot be maintained if it does not work—that is, if no one, not even those in power, is benefiting from it. How many times in history have less civilized nations conquered more civilized ones only to be entirely transformed by the cultural influence of their victims? Do we then feel ourselves to be less civilized than the Soviet Union? Is our system so brittle and theirs so enduring?

Actually, quite the contrary seems to be the case. For while democracy seems to be on a fairly sturdy basis in the United States (despite the efforts of self-appointed vigilantes to subvert it), there is considerable evidence that autocracy is beginning to decay in the Soviet Union.

Soviet Drift

Most Americans have great difficulty in evaluating the facts when they are confronted with evidence of decentralization in the Soviet Union, of relaxation of repressive controls, or of greater tolerance for criticism. We seem bewildered. And we do not seem to sense the contradiction when we say that these changes were made in response to public discontent. For have we not also believed deeply that an authoritarian regime, if efficiently run, can get away with ignoring the public's clamor?

There is a secret belief among us that Khrushchev must have been made to relax his grip in this way, or a contradictory suspicion that it is all part of a secret plot to throw the West off guard: a plot which is too clever for naive Americans to fathom. It is seldom suggested that "de-Stalinization" took place because the rigid, repressive authoritarianism of the Stalin era was inefficient, and that many additional relaxations will be forced upon the Soviet Union by the necessity of remaining amenable to technological innovation.

But the inevitable Soviet drift toward a more democratic structure is not dependent on the realism of leaders. Leaders come from communities and families, and their patterns of thought are shaped by their experiences with authority in early life, as well as by their sense of what the traffic will bear. We saw that the roots of American democracy were to be found in the nature of the American family. What does the Russian family tell us in this respect?

Pessimism regarding the ultimate destiny of Soviet political life has always been based on the seemingly fathomless capacity of the Russian people for authoritarian submission. Their tolerance for autocratic rulers was only matched by their autocratic family system which was equal to the German, the Chinese, or that of many Latin countries in its demand for filial obedience. On this early experience in the family the acceptance of authoritarian rule was based.

Role of the Family

But modern revolutionary movements, both facist and communist, have tended to regard the family with some suspicion, as the preserver of old ways and as a possible refuge from the State. Fascist dictators have extolled its conservatism but tended at times to set up competitive loyalties for the young. Communist revolutionaries, on the other hand, have more unambivalently attacked family loyalty as reactionary, and deliberately undermined familial allegiances, partly to increase loyalty to the state, and partly to facilitate industrialization and modernization by discrediting traditional mores.

Such destruction of authoritarian family patterns is a two-edged sword, which eventually cuts away political autocracy as well as the familial variety. The state may attempt to train submission in its own youth organizations, but so long as the family remains as an institution, this earlier and more enduring experience will outweigh all others. And if the family has been forced by the state to be less authoritarian, the result is obvious.

In creating a youth which has a knowledge, a familiarity, and a set of attitudes more appropriate for successful living in the changing culture than those of its parents, the autocratic state has created a Frankensteinian monster which will eventually sweep away the authoritarianism in which it is founded. Russian attempts during the late 1930's to reverse their stand on the family perhaps reflect some realization of this fact. Khruschev's denunciations of certain Soviet artists and intellectuals also reflect fear of a process going beyond what was originally intended. . . .

Further, what the derogation of parental wisdom and authority has begun, the fierce drive for technological modernization will finish. Each generation of youth will be better adapted to the changing society than its parents are. And each generation of parents will feel increasingly modest and doubtful about overvaluing its wisdom and superiority as it recognizes the brevity of its usefulness.

Conclusion

We cannot, of course, predict what forms democratization might take in any nation of the world, nor should we become unduly optimistic about its impact on international relations. Although our thesis predicts the ultimate democratization of the entire globe, this is a view so long-range as to be academic. There are infinite opportunities for global extermination before any such stage of development can be achieved.

We should expect that, in the earlier stages of industrialization, dictatorial regimes will prevail in all of the less developed nations, and as we well know, autocracy is still highly compatible with a lethal if short-run military efficiency. We may expect many political grotesques, some of them dangerous in the extreme, to emerge during this long period of transition, as one society after another attempts to crowd the most momentous social changes into a generation or two, working from the most varied structural base lines.

But barring some sudden decline in the rate of technological change, and on the (outrageous) assumption that war will somehow be eliminated during the next half century, it is possible to predict that after this time democracy will be universal. Each revolutionary autocracy, as it reshuffles the family structure and pushes toward industrialization, will sow the seeds of its own destruction, and democratization will gradually engulf it. Lord Acton once remarked about Christianity that it isn't that people have tried it and found it wanting. It is that they have been afraid to try it and found it impossible. The same comment may have once applied to democracy, but the outlook has changed to the point where people may *have* to try it.

We may, of course, rue the day. A world of mass democracies may well prove homogenized and ugly. It is perhaps beyond human social capacity to maximize both equality and understanding, on the one hand, and diversity, on the other. Faced with this dilemma, however, many people are willing to sacrifice quaintness to social justice, and we might conclude by remarking that just as Marx, in proclaiming the inevitability of communism, did not hesitate to give some assistance to the wheels of fate, so our thesis that democracy represents the social system of the electronic era should not bar these persons from giving a little push here and there to the inevitable.

Chapter Seven

The Peace Corps — A Case in Point

The creation of the Peace Corps in the summer of 1961 carried out President Kennedy's inaugural appeal for a generation of Americans to defend freedom "in its hour of maximum danger." The celebrated maxim, "And so, my fellow Americans: ask not what your country can do for you — ask what you can do for your country" was a summons to pursue again the American democratic mission. With his very special sense of history, the youthful President enlarged the scope of liberty and summoned all freedom-loving people to a common enterprise. "My fellow citizens of the world: ask not what America will do for you, but what together we can do for the freedom of man."

We have selected as a case study the Peace Corps, which brings students together with other kinds of citizens in a test of our larger ideological concern: Is American democracy exportable? A few years of Corps operations is hardly history; nevertheless, initial skepticism about the corpsmen being "junior" missionaries, ambassadors, or just visible democrats, has turned restless energies and a treasury of millions into a huge experiment in ideological contagion. The task of these volunteers, with their individual skills and common democratic faith, is made considerably harder by the troublesome mixtures of ideology with practicality, propaganda with education, modern methods with traditional habits. Can the United States aid other nations without insisting upon the cardinal American attitudes of faith in individual work, belief in progress, respect for science and education, the protection of liberties, limited government, minority rights, and equality of opportunity? The Corps is a part of our State Department, and is not conducted under any international authority. Although it brings people together wherever it operates, can the Corps really be free of any ideological purpose? Of one thing we can be sure: the inevitable interplay of learned behaviors, both individual and collective, will change the significance and perhaps the meaning of questions about the exportability of American democracy.

Hearings before the Senate Committee on Foreign Relations (1961)

The Peace Corps Act

(S. 2000, 87th Congress, Sess. I.)

A BILL to provide for a Peace Corps to help the peoples of interested countries and areas in meeting their needs for skilled manpower.

Be it enacted by the Senate and House of Representatives of the United States of America in Congress assembled,

Short Title

SECTION 1. This Act may be cited as the "Peace Corps Act."

Declaration of Purpose

SEC. 2. The Congress of the United States declares that it is the policy of the United States and the purpose of this Act to promote world peace and friendship through a Peace Corps, which shall make available to interested countries and areas and to international organizations men and women of the United States qualified for service abroad and willing to serve under conditions of hardship to help the peoples of such countries and areas in meeting their needs for manpower; to provide broader opportunities for men and women of the United States and United States private organizations, through service abroad, to contribute actively to their country's efforts in the cause of world peace and friendship; and through the service abroad of the men and women participating in Peace Corps programs, to promote a better understanding of the American people on the part of the peoples served. . . .

The Hearings

THE CHAIRMAN. Our first witness is Mr. Robert Sargent Shriver, Jr., who has been serving as Director of the Peace Corps established on a temporary basis by the President.

Mr. Shriver, we are glad to have you here. I believe you are accompanied by Mr. Moyers and several other of your aides. You have a prepared statement?

MR. SHRIVER. Yes, Mr. Chairman, I do.

THE CHAIRMAN. You may proceed, please, sir. . . .

The Peace Corps as Representative of American Idealism

Mr. Chairman and members of the committee, one month ago in India, Ashadevi, an extraordinary woman and former associate of the late Mahatma Gandhi, traveled three days and nights on a train to come to New Delhi to talk with me about the Peace Corps.

"Yours was the first revolution," she said. "Do you think young Americans possess the spiritual values they must have to bring the spirit of that revolution to our country? There is a great valuelessness spreading around the world and in India, too. . . . Your Peace Corps volunteers must bring more than science and technology. They must touch the idealism of America and bring that to us, too. Can they do it?"

This, Mr. Chairman, is the important question being asked not only abroad but in this country as well: Can we do it?

Three and one-half months ago we set out to try to answer that question. In defining our objectives we relied heavily, of course, on the President's message to the Congress on the Peace Corps. The recommendations he made have stood up under the test of our experiences to date. Three of his major points have become increasingly clear as primary objectives for our work.

Temporary Infusion of Manpower to Help Alleviate Shortages

First, the Peace Corps can furnish trained manpower to bring needed skills to the service of other countries. We learned that the missing link in these newly developing nations is often for "middle manpower"—men and women to do jobs until local people can be trained to take on this work themselves.

Ultimately, of course, education is the answer to the problems these nations face. They want neither charity nor handouts; what they seek is the brainpower, economic capacity, and political stability to work out their own salvations. But the process of education, especially in a new society, is long and slow, and there are important jobs to be filled before that process can produce enough trained people. In one west African country, for example, secretaries to some of the government ministers are young women from France who have come to fill these positions, because too few Africans are trained as stenographers, typists, or clerks. Critical shortages exist in almost every profession and every skill—in health, education, agriculture, business, government, and labor. One objective of the Peace Corps is to provide a temporary infusion of manpower to help meet those shortages.

Increased Awareness of the Situation in Underdeveloped Areas

A second and equally important objective is to give Americans an opportunity to learn more about life in a non-Western society and then to come home to share that knowledge with their fellow citizens. What is happening in the underdeveloped half of the world is of crucial importance to the role of the United States in world affairs today. Yet the American public is generally uninformed about the revolution taking place in societies where customs and traditions are in ferment. It is possible that the Peace Corps can help to build a constituency of Americans with a firsthand knowledge of what is happening in these countries.

Opportunity for Recipient Countries to Learn More About America

Third, the Peace Corps hopes to give people in other countries an opportunity to learn more about America through the experience of living and working with Americans. Let me illustrate what I mean by quoting from a letter one of the members of the Peace Corps staff received from a friend in Pakistan:

> The success of your Peace Corps will depend not primarily on the link between the U.S. Government and my Government, but between your people and our people, a link created by a surer understanding of the beliefs, languages, temperament, and, as a whole, the individual national aims. One cannot understand or know his neighbor unless he visits him in his home, shares his views, understands his wants or desires, and allows a friendship to grow through mutual respect and regard, irrespective of caste, color, or creed.

Steps Taken to Develop a Realistic Program

The policy of the Peace Corps is for its volunteers to live a simple existence, allowing the greatest possible spirit of partnership and cooperation with the people with whom he works.

There is a great difference, however, between a noble idea, such as this one, no matter how well conceived, and the execution of the idea in practical, realistic, down-to-earth terms.

As far as the Peace Corps was concerned, it was clear we had to get convincing answers to three important aspects of our problem in developing a viable, realistic Peace Corps program.

First, we had to know whether there was a genuine demand for Peace Corps services abroad. In other words, was there a market for the product we were intending to produce?

Second, was there an adequate supply of raw material, namely the manpower we would try to mold into Peace Corps volunteer workers?

Third, could we be sure that we could carefully screen and select, and then rigorously train, the personnel we would send abroad under the aegis of the Peace Corps?

We have given a great deal of time, thought, and energy to finding the answers to these important questions. Today I think I can report to you with confidence that in each case the answer is "Yes."

Existence of a Demand for Peace Corps Volunteers

In the first place, with respect to demand, we asked ourselves: Do other countries want, and will they welcome, Peace Corps volunteers? That demand soon became self-evident. Let me explain what I mean.

In response to invitations and expressions of interest on the part of leaders in Africa and Asia, I visited eight countries last month to discuss the Peace Corps. Prime Minister Nehru, of India, expressed a desire for agricultural extension workers to help meet his country's staggering need for food. Prime Minister Nkrumah, of Ghana, asked for plumbers, teachers, and electricians. He particularly wanted teachers—teachers of science and mathematics and many other subjects, teachers for his elementary schools and secondary schools and his universities as well.

President Garcia in the Philippines asked us to send teachers aides to help bolster the teaching of English, his country's national language. Prime Minister U Nu of Burma wanted health workers—sanitation engineers, nurses and nurses aides, medical technicians, doctors. And in all the other countries the needs were similar and urgent.

A recent cable from one country set forth its request for Peace Corps volunteers. The Ministries of Agriculture, Industry, Health, and Education in this country were asking—to mention only a few specific skills—for 8 agricultural administration office managers, 4 surveyors, 4 teachers in horticulture and soil research, 8 agricultural teacher trainers, 5 laboratory technicians, 50 nurses, 2 business administrators, and 2 economists. This cable was only one of a number of similar requests.

There is no doubt that an immense demand exists for talented Americans to do needed jobs in other countries.

The gap exists in the middle level for people who have skill and are willing to work hard. Requests are coming in every day for men and women with college, university, and professional training, for teaching, craft, art, farming, organizing, and leadership skills. Rather than advise and counsel the local people on how to accomplish their jobs, Peace Corps volunteers will go to help do the work and in the process will teach local people to do it themselves.

Ability, Availability, and Willingness of Sufficient Qualified Americans

Next came the question of supply. Are there enough qualified Americans available and willing to spend two years in a tough assignment abroad?

We think the answer is "Yes." In the first place, we have received about 11,000 completed applications.

Almost 4,000 Americans of all ages took the first battery of Peace Corps examinations—despite the fast that the tests were given during final examination periods on many college and university campuses and despite the fact that our tests are purely voluntary—1,500 took a second battery of tests. And we confidently expect an additional number at Peace Corps examinations in July, because we have been receiving more than 100 new applications a day all through May and June.

There is another barometer of the response the Peace Corps has been getting: An analysis of the first 4,800 eligible questionnaires. These interesting figures turn up: 712 applicants have professional skills in operating tractor equipment; 172 can run a bulldozer; there were 616 people with professional skills as carpenters, 205 as surveyors, 205 as electricians, 193 as masons, and 196 in metalworking; 370 applicants had professional experience with biology lab equipment and 473 with chemical lab equipment; 270 were professional nurses.*

Of the 4,800 applicants, 1,817 were college graduates and 1,203 persons had one or more years of graduate work; 1,000 of them can speak Spanish and another thousand can speak French.

But those are just statistics. What of the flesh and blood behind them?

Individual Recruits as Examples of Quality of Volunteers

I hope some of you may have read the newspaper accounts this week describing the first Peace Corps volunteers selected for training for projects in Tanganyika† and Colombia. I was impressed by the quality of those young men. I hope you were, too. I would like to call your attention to some of the persons who were selected.

Peter Von Christierson is a 28-year-old Californian who is a graduate student of engineering at the University of North Carolina. He received his bachelor's degree in civil engineering from the University of Colorado and was a student counselor there, working in a project involving the discipline and morale of 120 students.

Peter DeSimone of Connecticut is 24 and employed as a structural draftsman for the New York, New Haven & Hartford Railroad. He has worked as an apprentice carpenter on frame building construction in Bridgeport.

Gary Gaffner, who is 26 and a native of the state of Washington, has a bachelor of science degree in engineering and a master's degree in business administration from Stanford University. He has been a cost accountant, engineer, and sheet metal worker. He spent two years in the Army as a lieutenant and traveled in 92 countries.

---

*About 10,000 were serving in 1965 in 46 different countries. (Indonesia withdrew in 1965.)

†Now Tanzania.

He has been active in Little League baseball, Boy Scouts, and YMCA work.

Don Preston is a 23-year-old surveyor from Michigan. Arthur Young is 28 and has worked as a civil engineer on highway design. Charles Barton, 25 years old, is employed by the U.S. Forest Service as a surveying instrument man in the construction of forest roads. He already has experience as a full survey crew chief.

These are but a few of those who have been chosen and I single them out only because they are representative of the kind of competent, well-trained volunteer we are getting in the Peace Corps.

Adequacy of Peace Corps Training Program—Example of Tanganyikan Project

I come now to the third important problem we faced in organizing the Peace Corps: Once good volunteers have been recruited, can we train them to do a needed job in a foreign country and to represent the best of American life in the countries where they serve?

Perhaps I can answer that by describing the training program that will begin Monday in El Paso, Texas, at Texas Western College, for the surveyors and engineers who will go to Tanganyika to survey feeder roads for that Government.

The schedule begins at 5:30 every morning and ends at 9 P.M., six days a week. It includes studies in the culture of Tanganyika—its history, people, institutions, and traditions—plus medical training, courses in American studies, technical training, and physical conditioning.

Volunteers will study state highway specifications for different types of highways and terrain conditions. There will be reviews of soil theory and practice with emphasis on their use for drainage, base construction, and surfacing materials.

Special emphasis will be given to design and construction of small bridges, grading and maintenance of culverts and drains, and other similar problems the volunteer will face in Tanganyika. We are proud of the fact that the Texas Highway Department division office is cooperating to the fullest extent possible in this project. Four experts in their own areas of highway construction will assist Texas Western staff members in the instruction programs.

Courses in international affairs will include studies of Communist theories and techniques, nationalism in Africa, and other specific issues which may confront the volunteer in his work.

These procedures—and others which I have not mentioned for lack of time—are designed to give Peace Corps volunteers the best possible orientation for their assignments. We want men and women who will succeed because they are physically, mentally, and spiritually fit to work with their heads, their hands, and their hearts in strange environments and under difficult circumstances.

Cooperation with Experienced Individuals and Groups

In our attempts to find the answers to these questions we have had the best possible cooperation from the experienced men and women in private life who have operated overseas programs for voluntary, nonprofit agencies or for academic institutions. We have enjoyed the encouraging support and cooperation of various agencies of our own government and foreign governments as well.

And—I might add—we have had some very enlightening assistance from various members of Congress, their staffs, and the committees.

Substantial Peace Corps Endeavors To Be Carried Out through Universities and Voluntary Agencies

In carrying out our Peace Corps program we hope to utilize American universities and private voluntary agencies to the maximum. We have already had successful contacts resulting in actual agreements with a number of American universities and voluntary agencies including some of the most distinguished in our country. This initial experience encourages us to believe that we shall be successful in mounting a substantial proportion of our total effort through universities and voluntary agencies, and thereby avoid the creation of another large governmental bureau.

Request for Congressional Support of S. 2000

We have come here today to ask your support for a new bill that will enable us to carry forward the work which we have begun on a pilot basis at the request of the President. We are ready to try to answer your questions as ably as we can, but I hope you will share in my conviction that there are some questions about the Peace Corps that only time and experience will answer. On this occasion and in subsequent discussions we shall do our best to respond to your inquiries as clearly and succinctly as we can.

We in the Peace Corps feel a strong sense of responsibility to Congress and through Congress to the American people. We want to give an honest and faithful accounting of our stewardship to you and to your constituents.

Peace Corps Problems and Promise

We are under no illusions, Mr. Chairman. We know the Peace Corps is no panacea for all the ills of the world in general, or for any country in particular. We know there are problems ahead just as there is promise.

On the Great Seal of the United States is the date "1776" and an unfinished pyramid—a symbol which indicates that the task of extending human freedom and dignity is never done. We hope the Peace Corps can play a small part in this never-ending task. Our efforts will be successful if we can add in some small way to the growth of human freedom and dignity in the world.

Newspaper Stories Regarding Participation of Religious Groups in Peace Corps Activities

THE CHAIRMAN. Thank you, Mr. Shriver.

Mr. Shriver, I have noticed one or two editorials and accounts on the relationship of the Peace Corps to religious groups; I think this would be a good opportunity for you to clear up the questions they raise.

There was an article in the *New York Times* that I am sure you are familiar with. It is entitled "Any Church Role in Corps Decried." It says:

> A major Protestant denomination and the American Jewish Congress protested to the Peace Corps yesterday against the signing of oversea contracts with religious groups. . . .

MR. SHRIVER. Well, Mr. Chairman, in all of our literature and all of our public statements to date we have made it clear that the Peace Corps is not sending volunteers abroad to engage in religious activities. They are being sent abroad to assist other countries in meeting their needs for skilled manpower.

Therefore, we are not going to permit volunteers to engage in proselytizing or propagandizing for religious purposes.

The Peace Corps, of course, like any other federal agency, abides by the provisions of the First Amendment which prevents the Government from interfering with the free exercise of individual religious beliefs. We are certainly not going to tell the volunteers that they may not attend a church of their choice and participate in its activities in the same normal way that they do at home.

The Peace Corps is not going to provide funds to enable religious organizations to organize groups or to conduct church services or to proselytize in any other way, nor will we permit the volunteer to proselytize or recruit persons for religious services or preach on behalf of religious institutions. . . .

Purpose of the Peace Corps

SENATOR HICKENLOOPER. Mr. Chairman, may I ask a question on that point?

THE CHAIRMAN. Yes.

SENATOR HICKENLOOPER. Is your purpose in the Peace Corps to get information and assistance to countries, or is it to impose American ideals or ideas on other countries? In other words, if we say that we will impress American philosophy on these countries, then I can understand your refusal to make contracts with certain countries.

But if your purpose is to assist the countries, then why not, in furtherance of that assistance, send people that will be acceptable, and bow to their particular, and probably very deep-seated, beliefs that you and I may not agree with at all. I do not quite follow the philosophy here.

MR. SHRIVER. Well, the philosophy, Senator, is that we do not enter into agreements with organizations which have standards that are unacceptable to the Congress or to the American people.

For example, if, as I said, a religious organization insists on the right to proselytize, to try to get converts for its group, we will not enter into an agreement with them.

SENATOR HICKENLOOPER. That is not what I am talking about.

MR. SHRIVER. In the example of a foreign country, if they say, "We would be happy to have your people irrespective of race or creed, provided they did not propagandize or proselytize," we would consider that proposition very seriously, and might enter into it.

Frankly, Senator, we have not had any request insisting on religious restrictions and, in general, we refrain from making policy decisions based on hypothetical situations. We wait until we have a specific, concrete proposal from a particular country or organization, and then we decide on the basis of the merits of that case.

SENATOR HICKENLOOPER. Well, that still is not quite what I am trying to get an answer on.

MR. SHRIVER. Well, the purpose of our organization, Senator, as you very carefully and ably stated it, is to assist foreign countries, but we have to assist them on terms which we are able to meet.

Relationship of Peace Corps Assistance to Religious and Political Attitudes of Other Countries

SENATOR HICKENLOOPER. Let us get down to a concrete case. You and I do not agree with the attitude and the position taken by the Arab countries on excluding Jews, and I suppose most people in this country don't agree with that attitude. But is our purpose to assist the people of Arab countries? If so, why not send people who will be acceptable to them? Or is it our purpose to bring compulsion to bear, to have them change their basic attitude to one that conforms with our philosophy, religion, and so forth?

MR. SHRIVER. Of course, we are not trying to impose our opinions on them, but refraining from sending people there does not constitute, in my judgment, imposing our opinions on them.

In the second place———

SENATOR HICKENLOOPER. Well, you place certain standards which are not standards of help, but are standards of religious and political attitudes.

MR. SHRIVER. Well, for example, our———

SENATOR HICKENLOOPER. I am just trying to find out what it is you are trying to do here.

MR. SHRIVER. Of course, it is not quite altogether accurate that all of the Arab countries do not permit Jews to come to those countries. As we all know, there are———

SENATOR HICKENLOOPER. Some of them that do.

MR. SHRIVER (*continuing*). A great number of them which do not, and, therefore, we cannot again make generalizations about what we would do in all of the Arab countries.

There are some countries in the Arab group that do permit Jews to come in, and who might, these countries might, make overtures to the Peace Corps.

Let me repeat, we have not had any requests so far from such countries, and we are going, Senator, only where we are asked to go. We are not trying to go anywhere, certainly we are not trying to impose our beliefs on anybody. We are only going where we are asked.

. . . .

Minneapolis Star *Editorial Concerning Relationship of Peace Corps Policy to Views of Arab States*

THE CHAIRMAN. Mr. Reporter, in order that the record may be complete, I would like you to insert the entire editorial from the *Minneapolis Star*.

I wish to call attention to the fact that the *Minneapolis Star*, as I said, is one of the leading papers, and would represent, I think, a responsible attitude among men of the stature of Mr. Elston. In the last paragraph of his letter to me, he said:

> It would be disappointing if the Peace Corps were used to enforce our views on such controversial issues on states which are not yet ready and willing to accept such views of their own accord.

(*The editorial referred to follows.*)

A PEACE CORPS PROBLEM[1]

The Peace Corps, we are told, will not permit any discrimination against any of its members, or where they serve, on the basis of their race, color or religion.

Admirable as this policy is as an objective, it may serve to deny the benefits of Peace Corps projects to some of the Arab countries of the Middle East.

Arab governments, which regard all Jews as Zionists, supporters of Israel, and therefore their enemies, in a number of cases have refused to permit U.S. State and Defense Department personnel to serve at American installations within those countries, and thus could be expected to avoid the Peace Corps so long as such a policy prevails.

As a national aim, the Peace Corps policy is commendable. As a practical matter, we wonder whether the Peace Corps is the proper means for the United States to use in attacking such discrimination. For it is highly unlikely that the policy will change the Arabs' view and thus it simply will prevent the corps from performing badly needed tasks in some of the undeveloped lands of the Middle East.

In a recent speech, R. Sargent Shriver, Jr., the Peace Corps Director, said that 24 of the first 4,800 Peace Corps applicants could speak Arabic. It would be disappointing if these applicants could not be assigned to a country in which they could use their language ability.

It is true, of course, that the problem would be solved if the Arabs ended their discrimination against the Israelis and Jews elsewhere throughout the world. But since that is an unlikely prospect, does the U.S. Government serve the humanitarian purposes of the Peace Corps by insisting that the Arab countries adopt its point of view on this issue?

THE CHAIRMAN. I think you should consider that very seriously. We have had somewhat similar controversies in the Senate in connection with other legislation. While I think the statement of policy that you read is a correct statement, there is a great deal of difference of opinion as to whether or not we use aid legislation or, in this case, the Peace Corps legislation, to achieve other motives or purposes, that is, purposes other than aid.

[1] From the *Minneapolis Star* (June 19, 1961).

It is not entirely the same thing to state our own views as to what constitutes a proper course of action, and then use any form of assistance as an inducement for other people to change their views.

I think the Senator from Iowa was expressing very much the same point as the editor of the *Minneapolis Star*.

Does the Senator from Minnesota wish to question the witness?

Should Recipient Countries Impose Religious or Racial Qualifications for Volunteers?

SENATOR HUMPHREY. Let me just comment a bit on the *Minneapolis Star*. I have read it for a number of years. It is a very good newspaper, but I do not happen to agree with the position taken by my longtime friend, Mr. Elston.

I do not believe that you, sir, ought to impose religious qualifications for the recruitment of your personnel, and I do not believe you ought to have other countries impose upon us, in case of a cooperative relationship about to be entered into, religious qualifications as the basis of our assistance. This is just one Senator's point of view, and I hold it rather strongly.

I am a cooperative man, but not when it comes to sacrificing what I consider to be a very important point of view. I protested, for example, when the Union of South Africa would not permit Americans of the Negro race who were on an aircraft carrier, supposedly on a good will tour, to come ashore.

I will continue to protest that kind of action. I do not think you are sending Jews, or Catholics, or Protestants, or agnostics, or whatever overseas. I understand that you are sending American citizens; isn't that the idea, Mr. Shriver?

MR. SHRIVER. That is correct, Senator, and we ask no question about their race or creed.

All we are asking for is their ability to do a successful job overseas. If they can do that job on the basis of the selection process and training, we are ready to send them.

SENATOR HUMPHREY. That is right.

Well, I think that, if you adhere to that proposition in the main, you will steer a rather steady course.

. . . .

Extent and Nature of Past Missionary Contributions

SENATOR HICKENLOOPER. During all these generations in which missionary activities in the fields of agriculture, medicine, health, religion, morals, and spiritual training have taken place all over the world, and especially in what we might call the less developed parts of the world, we have not yet brought these areas to a point of social and economic thinking which we believe to be a proper standard; isn't that correct?

MR. SHRIVER. Well, certainly there are parts of the world less developed than this country. But I know, Senator, that the efforts of the missionary groups in large numbers of these countries have made large contributions to their development. Many of the leaders in those countries have been educated in mission schools, for example, and I would hesitate to devalue the work of mission schools, for example, to our own country. Many of the leaders of the New African countries are products of mission schools, and they are very friendly to this country because of the training they received in these schools, so I think they have made a great contribution.

SENATOR HICKENLOOPER. Let's don't have any misunderstanding. I was not suggesting they have not made a great contribution. I think they have made a fantastic contribution under very difficult situations. I am only trying to get a perspective of the magnitude of this problem.

MR. SHRIVER. It is a big problem, I agree with you, Senator.

SENATOR HICKENLOOPER. For generations we have had tens of thousands of these dedicated people over the world, contributing their services, abilities, and lives. We have actually had a peace corps for generations, have we not?

MR. SHRIVER. Well, I would certainly—

Nature of the Peace Corps

SENATOR HICKENLOOPER. I mean, we have had for generations a corps for progress composed of these dedicated people who have gone out of the United States and been supported by institutions and private contributions and other methods.

My only point is: How are you going to revolutionize the world with the altruistic claims and statements that are so breathlessly made about the Peace Corps and what it can do with 2,000 or 3,000 comparatively untrained people who are going to take the banner of young Lochinvar and march forward, when this effort over the past several years, as great as it has been, has not completely brought these standards up? It is just a perspective, that is all.

MR. SHRIVER. Well, Senator, I guess, perhaps, I share your perspective, because I know of no member of my staff who has ever claimed that we were going to revolutionize the world, nor do we think we are going to change the world overnight or over a generation. All we are trying to do, Senator, is to make a contribution in the kind of worthwhile work that you seem to be in favor of.

SENATOR HICKENLOOPER. That we are now approaching the problem of underprivileged in the world with the Peace Corps has been presented as a great new philosophy, a great new idea. I am not saying I am necessarily going to oppose it or vote against it, but I would like to look at some of the fanfare that goes with it to see just what it is.

MR. SHRIVER. Well, Senator, I do not think that we have proposed that this is some great new idea. We have said, I think, or people have said, at any rate, that it probably is the first time when a government attempted to perform to help in this kind of work.

As a matter of fact, in our presentation on page 1 we say: "The basic concept of the Peace Corps is not new."

This is our presentation to the Congress. "It has been suggested that in its philosophical underpinning it may go back to William James in the early part of this century." . . .

These are our own statements, and we do not claim that it is a new idea. But I do think, Senator, that it is somewhat new for a government to be helping in this area. . . .

Certain Countries Viewed as Ineligible for Peace Corps Programs: Example of Cuba

SENATOR CHURCH. That brings me to the series of questions which the testimony until now has not clarified for me.

You have indicated that no Peace Corps program will be established in any country that does not ask for it.

MR. SHRIVER. Yes, sir.

SENATOR CHURCH. So the first requisite for the establishment of a Peace Corps program is that the host country asks for it?

MR. SHRIVER. That is right.

SENATOR CHURCH. Now suppose that Fidel Castro were to ask for the establishment of a Peace Corps program in Cuba, operators for tractors or something of that kind. (*Laughter.*)

Would you regard Cuba as eligible for this program? I do not want to put you on a spot, but I would like to get at the basis for these determinations. Would you regard Cuba today, under existing circumstances, or the Dominican Republic (under Dictator Trujillo), for that matter, as eligible for the Peace Corps program?

MR. SHRIVER. Well, Senator, our Peace Corps is an agency of the State Department and, therefore, we are under the direction of the Secretary of State as well, of course, as the President of the United States.

SENATOR CHURCH. So before establishing a program in any country the approval of the Secretary of State and of the President is first obtained?

MR. SHRIVER. Oh, definitely. When we get a project to this point where we think it has the possibilities of a viable program, it is then discussed with the appropriate officials of the State Department. Copies of it, as I explained this morning, are given to the desk officers, both in State and in ICA and informational copies go to the Assistant Secretaries of State and over to the USIA people, so that we do not actually conclude an agreement with any country until it has been well processed and gone over here. In the case of Cuba specifically I would be quite surprised if we undertook a program or contracted to undertake a program in a country that did not have diplomatic relations with us.

SENATOR CHURCH. I would, too. I think we would place those two countries in a special category.

. . . .

Peace Corps Not Viewed Primarily as an Economic Aid Program

MR. SHRIVER. ... It is possible, Senator, that it might be helpful and advisable for the Peace Corps to go into a country where there is no foreign aid program. As a matter of fact, one such country is under consideration now, and I believe that the State Department has indicated that they think it would be good for the Peace Corps to go into that country.

The Peace Corps is not primarily or certainly not solely an instrument of economic, of foreign economic, policy. In one country I had the temerity to suggest that it was possible that a number of Peace Corps people could serve in a particular country for a number of years and that the gross national product might go down. I do not think that we can equate Peace Corps operations with the economic requirements of a country. The Peace Corps is more of a cultural, an educational, and social operation than it is an economic one. So that it is possible that in some countries of advanced economic development, the Peace Corps could be very helpful.

There was some newspaper publicity within the last month relating to Japan, and it was indicated in Japanese newspapers and in ours here that Japan might request Peace Corps personnel.

Well, by no stretch of the imagination would I suppose could we say that Japan is an industrially underdeveloped country, yet it might be advisable for a variety of reasons for the Peace Corps to accept a request from the Japanese Government, if one were extended to us. That would be a decision again made not only by us but by other officials of the State Department. My point is simply this, that ours is not solely or primarily an economic aid program.

Value of Ambition

SENATOR CAPEHART. Let us not carry this to the point where the people over there say, "Well, there is no need for us to adopt the American system of government or the American way of life because it is not any better than ours." Let's not carry it too far by getting down to their level. Otherwise there will be little likelihood of their changing their system of government and improving themselves, if we are going to go over there and leave the impression that we are on a par with them or they are on a par with us.

MR. SHRIVER. Well, that is not the objective, of course.

SENATOR CAPEHART. I am sure it is not, but I say you might be able to carry that too far. I know I grew up as a poor boy, and my ambition was to make some money, and I had certain heroes around me whom I looked up to.

MR. SHRIVER. You see, this in substance—

SENATOR CAPEHART. I think if everybody had been on a par with me, and I had not been able to see people better dressed than I was, and who had more things than I did, I do not think I would have had the ambition to work as hard as I did.

MR. SHRIVER. Well, let me explain about, for example, the surveyors in Tanganyika. The Tanganyikan Government told us that the greatest number of surveyors that they could produce through their own educational system was two surveyors a year.

SENATOR CAPEHART. Yes.

MR. SHRIVER. And that, therefore, it would take them ten years to get twenty Tanganyikan surveyors.

Question of the Nature and Worth of Proposed Living Standards

SENATOR CAPEHART. I am highly in favor of that sort of thing, and that is the thought I want to convey to you. You are sending them over there to do a specific job and do it well, to mind their own business and to render a service to the people—something that can be seen and felt during the time the volunteers are there and after they leave. I do not quite go along with this idea that you have to live as they live and do as they do and dress as they dress, et cetera. I am not so sure that that is a good facet of your program. . . .

I think the best part of your program is that you are going to render a real service to the recipient countries. In other words, when a man or the group leaves there, the community is better off and the people can see and feel the accomplishments of the Corps.

I am not sure I am sold on the idea of reducing our people to their level because I do not believe that is good human psychology or a good human relationship, and I think that might well be a weakness in your program if you carry it too far, as I said a moment ago. I do not know why you have to carry it that far. If you are going to send a doctor over there, I would hope he would go over there and take out a lot of tonsils and adenoids, and cure several people, and render real service to them. The same thing applies to the nurses, and the surveyors, who will survey some roads and help build them.

If you carry this to an extreme—which you may well do—of hardship and reducing our people to living as they do in the underdeveloped countries, I am not opposed to it, but I just do not believe that is the way—knowing human nature as I think I do—to sell people on the idea of doing better, of imitating other people, and wishing to improve themselves. I am afraid you might fail if you carry it to an extreme.

. . . .

Need for Simplicity in the Peace Corps

SENATOR GORE. I shall not ask you any further questions, but I shall offer a brief opinion of my own, for whatever it may be worth, on the administration of this important program.

I think the success you may be able to obtain may be in direct ratio to the degree to which you can keep this program simple and direct to the people of the countries in which you operate. The foreign aid program has had difficulties in many instances, and is having many difficulties now, because of its identity with and close association with the particular regimes which happen to be in power.

As I understand your program, the heart and core of it, as was true of the point 4 program, is a people-to-people program, bringing the skills and talents of the people who, in good will, volunteer to contribute two years of their lives to this contest in which we seek the friendship of men. . . .

Suggestions Pertaining to the Nature and Operation of the Corps

MR. ROW. . . . Based on our own deep interest in the declared objectives of the Peace Corps, and growing out of our own experiences in these general types of service activities over several decades, we desire now, with your permission, to offer in somewhat categorical terms, several suggestions on the nature and operation of the Peace Corps.

1. The Peace Corps should never be used as an instrument of the cold war. Yet this temptation will be very great especially when it has its most pronounced successes. The Peace Corps is a creative,

challenging, even explosive idea. But it is inappropriate as a warhead, and when so used, it will turn out to be a dud, or even worse, a boomerang upon us as a people.

2. It follows that the Peace Corps should not be used as a front for partisan world politics, even our own. The Peace Corps will succeed only as it succeeds in meriting the enthusiasm and responsible participation of the people with whom and for whom it serves. The potential response will freeze in its tracks the moment people abroad see the Peace Corps as any kind of bait for any kind of trap. Certainly our experiences abroad as a nation these last years ought to sear this danger into our consciousness.

3. The Peace Corps posture should be lodged as fully as possible in international terms and organizations. The Achilles heel of the Peace Corps conceivably might be its nationalistic image abroad. Our own motives seem clear and idealistic to us. Even our friends abroad sometimes see them less favorably. The best guarantee against this charge of selfish motivation will be to internationalize the program in terms of policy, organization, personnel and projects. The United Nations should be involved much more in consultation and programing.

4. The Peace Corps should never cease emphasizing people-to-people values. This means more than lip service; it involves a steady deemphasis upon Government bureaucracy and redtape, both of which seem to be growing at a frightening rate in the present temporary Peace Corps agency. It means maximum use of the private and voluntary services of our Nation in definition of objectives, selection, and management of projects, recruitment and training of corpsmen, and in interpreting the Peace Corps to the American public. It means substantial use of younger and semi-skilled volunteers who can live in close, friendly, and helpful contact with simple village people.

Supplementary Reading List

In addition to the readings already cited, these few selections expand on various issues raised in the text. References to a growing list of journal articles, monographs and scholarly reports may also be found in the footnotes and chapter references in these books.

ALMOND, GABRIEL, and COLEMAN, JAMES. *The Politics of the Developing Areas.* Princeton: Princeton University Press, 1960.

ALMOND, GABRIEL, and VERBA, SIDNEY. *The Civic Culture.* Princeton: Princeton University Press, 1963.

BRYCE, JAMES B. *The American Commonwealth.* 2 vols. New York: The Macmillan Co., 1893.

BURNS, EDWARD M. *The American Idea of Mission: Concepts of National Purpose and Destiny.* New Brunswick, N.J.: Rutgers University Press, 1957.

EKIRCH, ARTHUR A., JR. *Ideas, Ideals, and American Diplomacy.* New York: Appleton-Century-Crofts, 1966.

HAMILTON, W. B. (ed.). *The Transfer of Institutions.* Durham, N.C.: Duke University Press, 1964.

HANDLIN, OSCAR (ed.). *American Principles and Issues: The National Purpose.* New York: Holt, Rinehart & Winston, Inc., 1961.

KOHT, HALVDAN. *The American Spirit in Europe: A Survey of Transatlantic Influences.* Philadelphia: University of Pennsylvania Press, 1949.

LERNER, MAX. *America as a Civilization.* New York: Simon and Schuster, Inc., 1957.

LILLIBRIDGE, GEORGE D. *Beacon of Freedom: The Impact of American Democracy Upon Great Britain, 1830-1870.* Philadelphia: University of Pennsylvania Press, 1955.

LIPSET, SEYMOUR MARTIN. *The First New Nation: The United States in Historical and Comparative Perspective.* New York: Basic Books, Inc., 1963.

———. *Political Man.* New York: Doubleday & Co., Inc., 1960.

MCGIFFERT, MICHAEL. *The Character of Americans.* Homewood, Ill.: The Dorsey Press, 1964.

MEAD, MARGARET. *Cultural Patterns and Technical Change.* Paris: United Nations, 1953.

MORGENTHAU, HANS J. *The Purpose of American Politics.* New York: Alfred A. Knopf, Inc., 1960.

PYE, LUCIAN. *Aspects of Political Development.* Boston: Little, Brown and Co., 1966.

PYE, LUCIAN, and VERBA, SIDNEY (eds.). *Political Culture and Political Development.* Princeton, N.J.: Princeton University Press, 1965.

RAPSON, RICHARD L. (ed.). *Individualism & Conformity in the American Character.* Boston: D. C. Heath & Co., 1967.

SHILS, E. (ed.). *Democracy In the New States.* New York: Paragon Book Gallery, 1959.

STROUT, CUSHING. *The American Image of the Old World.* New York: Harper & Row, 1963.

TOCQUEVILLE, ALEXIS DE. *Democracy in America.* Translated by PHILIPS BRADLEY. 2 vols. New York: Alfred A. Knopf, Inc., 1956.